LIFE
AFTER
DIVORCE

Create A New Beginning

Sharon Wegscheider-Cruse

Health Communications, Inc.
Deerfield Beach, Florida

Library of Congress Cataloging-in-Publication Data

Wegscheider-Cruse, Sharon
    Life after divorce: create a new beginning/Sharon Weg-
    scheider-Cruse.
        p.   cm.
    ISBN 1-55874-282-4 (pbk.): $8.95
    1. Divorce. 2. Divorce counseling. 3. Divorced people
    — Counseling of. I. Title.
HQ814.W44   1993   93-46943
306.89—dc20   CIP

©1994
ISBN 1-55874-282-4

Publisher: Health Communications, Inc.
            3201 S.W. 15th Street
            Deerfield Beach, Florida 33442-8190

Cover design by Barbara Bergman

**Other Books by
Sharon Wegscheider-Cruse**

*Another Chance:
Hope And Health For The Alcoholic Family*

*Choicemaking For Co-dependents,
Adult Children And Spirituality Seekers*

Learning To Love Yourself: Finding Your Self-Worth

Coupleship

The Miracle of Recovery

Understanding Co-dependence

Acknowledgments

I would especially like to thank Galadriel Mohan for her clear thoughts and interest in this book. My thanks to Barbara Nichols and Marie Stilkind for their special contributions. Always, I thank Peter Vegso and Health Communications for inviting me to publish, and especially Gary Seidler who kept nudging me until I got this book written.

Sharon Wegscheider-Cruse

I would like to dedicate this book to the many people who have chosen to "begin again." My life has been enriched by the courage, risks and compassion that I've seen in those who "choose new life."

Contents

1

Divorce Possibilities: Action Versus Fear

Divorce no longer carries its old stigma in our society but it hurts as much as ever. With the divorce rate as high as it is, few of us don't cringe, at least inwardly, when the word is mentioned. Most marriages have a tinder box with at least a few combustible issues. At frustrating times when our differences flare, just thinking about divorce may be a safety valve. But we're not serious. We'll keep the lid on and work out our problems — somehow.

Then the time comes when one half of a couple decides that solutions to the marital problems are not going to happen. Working it out has failed. *We* have failed. At least, that's how we feel.

So we divorce and the marriage is over. But divorce recovery has just begun.

Is it the end of the world? Or the beginning of a better world for us, in which peace, greater fulfillment and enhanced self-esteem aren't dreams but realities?

No one can doubt my response to that question. We're not only talking about divorce survival in this book. This is about taking hold of our experience and using it to turn our lives around.

THE EVENT OF DIVORCE

We're taking an event that some see as primarily negative and bending it into a life enhancer. As a result of divorce we're going to be learning so much about ourselves — and others — that we'll eventually say, "Divorce was one of the best things that ever happened to me!"

I did it. I came to a positive attitude about divorce. Many others have, too. All it takes is understanding, commitment and, most of all, action. The ability to change also helps.

There are no "victims" of divorce in the classic sense. There are only victims of the myth that divorce is something to feel guilty about or lose confidence over. Divorce prompts a wide range of feelings: relief, anger, hope, hopelessness, sadness, excitement, shame, regret, vengefulness, pity — and almost everything in between. Divorce is about the shattering of fondest hopes and fantasies about a life partner that didn't materialize. No wonder that recovering from all of this presents the challenge of a lifetime. But it is a challenge we can accept with so much help available to us in many forms, including the often underdeveloped source which is ourselves.

DIVORCE VARIABLES

There are many variables that impact each divorce. They include:

- Young children
- Older children
- Adult children
- Child support problems
- Alimony problems

- Custody problems
- Affairs and betrayals

In addition, there are a host of other issues. There are those supporters and criticizers among friends and rela tives. There are the different perspectives of a first divorce compared to a second divorce. There are even variables present when we are talking about either short-term marriages or long-term marriages. Then there is the "excess baggage" that we bring to a marriage from our childhood families or a previous marriage.

We could talk endlessly about how every variation complicates or simplifies divorce but the focus of this book is on *healing* from the trauma that divorce presents to us. Whatever they are, the forms are not insurmountable. Our concern is: Can *we* surmount them? We need to know we've got what it takes, and we need to learn why it's been hidden within us. How can we bring forth our remarkable latent capacities to cope and thrive? How can we live without a spouse and like it? How do we deal with the children, the relatives and the mutual friends? How do we keep from making other mistakes in relationships?

Our questions may be seriously tinged with self-doubt. Erasing this doubt will be our main goal.

In a perfect world, all marriages would succeed because we would all be psychic and aware of every present and future need of our own *and* our mate's. This book is not about promoting divorce as a *means* of growth, even though that is frequently the result. It *is* about releasing people from the past to pursue with confidence the new direction their personal lives are taking.

Society has been changing rapidly and radically. People change in response to it, and some marriages need to end as a result. If a divorce is going to happen, let's make it an event marking renewal, not useless regret.

In addition to my 20-plus years of working with couples and families, I have interviewed more than 200 divorced people to find out what the divorce recovery process felt like and ultimately meant to them. Some of these ex-spouses will be sharing their stories with us as we explore the challenges we face.

In talking to many people about what caused and contributed to their divorces, the number-one marriage killer was perceived to be a lack of basic emotional connection between husband and wife. When people were asked to be more specific, 90 percent said that one partner simply lost passion for the other.

Many of the people I interviewed said they sensed something was wrong quite early in the relationship. Half said that even though they knew something was wrong, they hung in there for four years or more, refusing to believe their marriages couldn't get better.

Here are the most frequent reasons for divorce among my surveyed ex-partners, starting with the most common problem:

1. Lack of emotional intimacy
2. Affection dissatisfaction
3. Work interference
4. Child-rearing disagreements
5. Husband's inability to accept wife's work outside the home
6. Husband's inability to make money
7. Infidelity
8. Sexual dissatisfaction
9. Boredom
10. Lack of friendship

Obviously, any of these is a serious problem to live with. No wonder *happiness* was the word agreed upon by half the people I surveyed in response to my question, "What emotion did you feel most often after divorcing?"

All too frequently, people afraid of divorce assume that divorced people are always lonely and depressed. And those who are lonely and depressed tend to think this is the way it has to be. As my survey shows, many people are in a position to view it as a life-affirming, self-affirming change — and we all can achieve that viewpoint! That's what this book is about.

One thing most of us learn from divorce is that the experience is far more than getting over a separation and getting used to living alone. That's jumping a step. For many, divorce introduces us to ourself, which for several years was at least partially hidden by adaptations to the needs and personality of someone else. Finding out what we would do and want, if we were free to choose, can be a little frightening. We've changed since before the beginning of our marriage when we were single. Who are we today? Worry about our new status can delay that discovery.

In all our post-divorce transactions, we need to concentrate on action more and imagining calamities less. "To thine ownself be true," Shakespeare said with good reason. When we cling to old images of ourselves or ideas of how others expect us to be, the outcome will never be positive. It's mainly through *doing something* about our situation that we learn how strong, how adaptable, how clever and how capable we really are. Convincing ourselves of our positive points just by imagining them doesn't work. If you don't know who you are, you won't know where you are going. But if you don't start going, you won't start finding out who you are.

A PRACTICAL BEGINNING

There are many very practical matters that need to be tackled in the beginning of divorce. However, don't let the momentum of your actions wind down after you have:

- agreed on decisions affecting children
- divided common property
- divided personal belongings

- changed wills and legal documents
- informed parents
- informed siblings
- informed friends
- chosen a good accountant
- arranged new telephone listings
- notified the post office
- separated the bank accounts
- dealt with the charge accounts
- redone the bedrooms and closets (more space!)

BECOMING SINGLE AGAIN

In this new time of being single, there are wonderful discoveries to be made. They include:

1. Finding out we are going to make it.
2. Finding out we can be on our own.
3. Finding out it is sort of nice to be in charge of all our time and activities.
4. Enjoying some solitude and serenity.

Some of the discoveries aren't so pleasant:

1. We miss having a meal with that person.
2. We wish there were someone to share day-to-day life with.
3. We find we keep running into certain sadnesses — some shortfalls and some habits we don't like — over and over again.
4. We don't have the other person to blame.
5. Eventually, we have to confront the fact that we alone are responsible for what is happening to us, and what is going to happen. No more leaning on another's life.

Full singleness does not occur at the same moment for both of the separating spouses. Both may be working at it, both in transition, but they end their process of divorce recovery at different times. Some people may remarry immediately. Some, eventually. Some are going to love being single and vow to never give up their in-charge feelings again. Comparing your feelings and actions to your ex-partner's or someone else's is not valid. We need to see ourselves as unique and on our own. Today, I myself am in a marriage that is fulfilling, challenging and of great value to me. There was a time when I did not believe this would ever happen to me. That was when I was living in the past.

If we are to be fully alive, we will actively live with changes our whole life. Things will not remain in static pain or static peace. Life is not like that. It is constantly moving, surrounded by movement. If you go with it, instead of trying to swim against the current, you can have a fantastic journey and adventure:

I release my past and former relationships. Today is the only day that really exists. The past is gone. The only place it exists is in my own thoughts. When I let the past become very powerful, the hurt of the past, the mistakes of the past — sometimes even the joys of the past — make me miss out on what's happening today.

There isn't anything that will make the past the present. Dwelling on it drains energy I could be using to focus on the present. I won't forget it but I will say goodbye to it. From what it has taught me, I will fashion a key to the future — a tool only to help me, not to hinder me. I'm not who I was yesterday; I'm not who I will be — but I'm getting there a day at a time — lighter and self-powered!

2

Dynamics
Of A
Dissolving
Marriage

Joan, Ken, Kathy and **Bob** experienced divorce from the perspectives of four different lives. At the start of each chapter we will follow their stories, from guilt, doubt and resentment, through the process of self-understanding to new lives of self-fulfillment.

> **Joan:** When I was first married, I admired my husband Alan's stability and calmness. He seemed unflappable, which was new to me in a man since my dad had been an alcoholic.
> I was a flexible person and we agreed on almost everything. His first marriage ended because his wife always challenged his preferences. This was never a problem with us, but in another way, I guess you could say it was.

9

Alan preferred that I forget my parents'
problems. I couldn't see why he didn't
understand that I had to do something for
them. Then the kids came along. They meant
more problems and less time. I became the one
who had to figure out how to deal with
everything while he retreated. I didn't think
much of this attitude, and I let him know it.
This was supposed to be a partnership. I got
counseling and learned to speak up.
He learned to play golf, but he wasn't
interested in counseling.

Ken: Amanda was really involved in the
town where we used to live. I guess I was a
little egotistical to think she'd follow me
anywhere, as the saying goes, but isn't that
what a marriage is about? Well, she followed
me but I guess she got even. Amanda was
always a good-looking woman, even after
three kids, but I really didn't expect her to get
involved with other guys. I was out there in
the business world, knocking myself out so we
could live in the right house, with the good
cars, best schools for our kids, and she . . .
   She could have been more subtle about it.
Her affairs just about killed me. Alcohol kept
my mind off what was going on. I wasn't ready
to concede that I had somehow missed the
mark, despite the trappings. We looked good
but we never had much to say to each other
about things that mattered. After we went to
counseling, we discovered our marriage didn't
really have enough glue to hold all the pretty
pieces together.

Kathy: How is it that what makes you attractive to your husband before marriage can turn him off after marriage? For a long time I couldn't figure that out. I tell my friends, "Stay attractive to your husbands or you'll lose them!" That's what I'd always heard and it made sense. There is a lot of competition out there, even after you're married. My mom was forever fixing herself up for Dad. It seems to work for her — they've been married 30 years!

Anyway, Jim knew I was a physical person. I was a cheerleader and he was a football player. He seemed real happy about my looks and talked about my great body. After we married, there was no way I was going to become a frumpy housewife. I went to aerobics class. I began running. I sort of got carried away. Looking better than most women made me feel more secure in my marriage. It even got us attention when we went out. But Jim started complaining about my time spent at classes. He said I was being self-centered. I still wonder how he expected me to stay in that shape without work.

Bob: I was born on the other side of the tracks and had to do a lot of bluffing to get where I am without going to college or having a supportive family behind me. I love traveling, meeting people, talking them into what's good for them — and me! Deena is a born homebody and I thought I needed that. She would be a sweet anchor.

We complemented each other at first, but as my career developed I needed more

understanding from her about my being away.
She knew I was faithful, so that was never a
problem. Later I could have used her help as a
hostess occasionally. I also expected some
respect for my friends. That's when I got into
drinking. And the alcohol set off sirens in her
head because alcohol was a problem in her
family, and suddenly she couldn't accept me
anymore.

MARITAL ASPECTS

When a relationship that once offered a secure haven of
comfort and warmth becomes a source of deep disappointment and depression, we often turn to blame to treat our
hurt. As betrayed spouses, we want it known just how
badly the other has misbehaved and just who is responsible
for spoiling the beautiful relationship we once shared.

After a while it becomes clear that our spouse will never
say, "You're right, after all." Most likely, both individuals
have decided that they speak two different languages. The
usual ways of communicating to solve problems don't work
anymore. The former lovers have taken up emotional res-
idence on distant planets, and from these remote fortresses
each one is firing recriminations at the other for causing
the loss of love. The other person is looked upon as a love
thief, someone who cheated and stole away the good life.

One party may cling to wishful thinking, but when a
marriage hits bottom it is clear to at least one spouse that
the marriage will never be like it once was. There is no
guarantee in life that people will change and grow in tan-
dem. Often when growth occurs, one spouse begins to
question "givens" built into the beginning of the marriage.
For example:

- "Why do I always have to discipline the kids?"
- "Do I have to be the one who takes care of his parents?"
- "Can't I have any friends she doesn't like?"

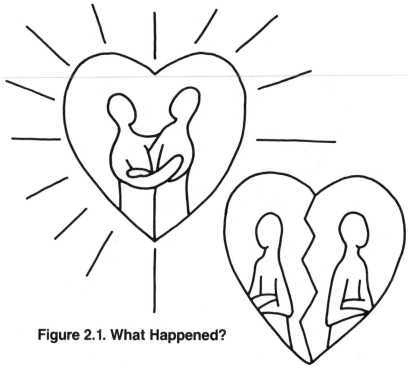

Figure 2.1. What Happened?

Perhaps one partner seeks a new horizon and the other panics: "I don't need this, why does she?" In recent years, many people have become involved in the search for self-knowledge and discovery. They've found that exploring their emotional lives has given them answers to old puzzles and dealing with the past resolves inner conflicts. But when they try to communicate their enthusiasm for disclosure of feelings with their partners, they may encounter resistance: "Why get into psychology?" or "Too much analysis can drive you crazy." The partners may see self-exploration as abandonment or betrayal, the "last straw" in a series of growing differences that are bewilderingly new and beyond their capacity to cope.

COMPATIBILITY'S DOWN SIDE

Usually, compatibility is a big plus in marriage, but often it can work against communication. If two people share the *compatibility of openness,* they have a good shot at being able to resolve conflict. People who don't hide their feelings much from others tend not to hide much from themselves. Listening to others speak their minds isn't so scary because they are used to processing their own uncomfortable, as well as comfortable, feelings. They can identify with self-disclosure. They don't have to tune out when emotions rise. They will try to feel the other's feelings as well as hear them.

However, if a couple shares the *compatibility of defensiveness,* they may appear to live in harmony but this is only because they aren't really facing reality. Sharing the same defensive pattern, they run for cover when they identify a sticky issue. Ultimately, their union may become a rigid citadel through which cold winds blow, chilling their hearts.

Disaster strikes and distance grows when one partner is moved through desperation to change or to seek the warmth of more openness.

When two people seem to grow apart in love, it's usually only one who is growing.

ELEMENTS OF EROSION: FLASH POINTS OF A MARRIAGE BREAKDOWN

The poet Thomas Campbell may have felt " 'Tis distance lends enchantment to the view," but in relationships, moments of feeling distant from your love are not the enchantment you had hoped to have in your marriage. Often they are the telltale signs that your spouse is a different kind of person from the one you bargained for. Sometimes it takes a string of these events to realize that they were turning points. You were being compelled by them to see the marriage in a new way. At these times, both persons often could feel that something was wrong, but the threat was so great that the incidents were not given the significance they achieved in hindsight.

These moments don't usually spring out of thin air or come as the result of unusual major traumas, but occur instead during life changes we all experience. These changes are often ordinary stressful events. How we respond to them highlights our emotional strengths or weaknesses. Attitudes we may have concealed, either intentionally or unintentionally, are in full view and must be dealt with by our partners. If we are "in sync" and understanding prevails, we weather change together. If our response is too "foreign" to the value system or response level of our partner, alarms go off.

Some of the stressful events that may send up smoke signals occur when:

1. Either spouse starts a college program
2. A new job is begun
3. A move to a new city is necessary
4. A child is born
5. A parent dies
6. A one-career family expands to two careers, or a two-career family shrinks to one career
7. One or both partners retire
8. A child becomes seriously ill
9. Children graduate from grade school to high school to college
10. Children leave home.

Three more pivotal points, less specific and often quite subtle, can spark deep-seated differences. They are:

1. When unshared interests draw the couple apart
2. When one partner loses respect for the other
3. When one spouse begins to conceal feelings

A "COUPLESHIP"

There are, of course, many more situations that can reveal hidden or dormant attitudes and lead to shifts in relationships. As easily as they can separate people, these events also offer the opportunity for couples to draw closer together, but only if their channels of communication are wide open. The ability to communicate offers the possibility of negotiating different responses than those that can destroy a "coupleship."

Several years ago, I developed a couple's program that continues today as a five-day event. It offers couples an opportunity to explore the dynamics of their relationship. A term grew out of these experiences: *coupleship*. I define it as a passionate, spiritual, emotional/sexual commitment between two people that nurtures both of them and maintains a high regard for the value of each person.

Anyone can have a one-sided relationship with another person, place, substance or event. It is a dynamic process of a person relating to a parent, friend, pet, possession or job. As such, it is a one-sided attachment.

A coupleship, however, is two people *choosing* to have a relationship with each other and the investment in building and strengthening that union.

PARTNERSHIP ALERTNESS

Alertness to what might be significant in the life of your partner is another factor that keeps relationships from sliding into hopelessness. In our busy and active lives, it is easy just to focus on what bothers us and forget that other people might react differently to events we take for granted. A relationship can erode slowly but steadily through neglect so that all it takes is one pivot point to spin it out of control.

TRAUMA: THE POINT OF UNLIKELY RETURN

More obvious direct hits to a troubled marriage are the major traumatic events that may affect one or both of the partners. These events cause relationship damage that seems "too great to heal." Examples of this type of trauma might be:

1. Exposure of a partner's affair
2. Death of a child
3. Bankruptcy
4. Betrayal
5. Mismanagement of money
6. Serious or chronic health issues
7. Preoccupation with child rearing
8. Overextending oneself professionally (workaholism)

Usually when a traumatic event occurs, it has been preceded by a history of problems that needed only one torpedo to finish sinking the matrimonial ship. In a partnership where there is commitment — together with the willingness to face anger, hurt, grief and vulnerability — trauma has less chance of doing irreparable damage. Trauma can actually bring a couple closer together as they find comfort in one another and mount a joint effort to find solutions to ease the pain.

Well-cemented relationships contain two people who are consistently and constantly involved in emotional home maintenance. They are attentive to what they are each becoming and how they are interacting with others.

GROWING CLOSER

Commonality is the glue that sticks people together who stay together. They are committed to creating common friends, a joint home, common hobbies and, sometimes, raising children together. The couple has a common future and within their vision they continue to define themselves as a couple. Those around them think of them together as a twosome, not as individuals with shadowy spouses in the background. These people are together not because they don't want to be alone but because they want to enhance their life by sharing it with *this* person.

Good relationships involve two factors: what is happening between a couple as two people and how they, both as individuals and as a couple, relate to the world around them.

In the words of Virginia Satir: "Peace and harmony will come when people pay attention to peace within (individuals), peace between (couples) and peace among (families)."

GROWING APART

Often before anyone notices from outside of the marriage, when a coupleship begins to erode or disintegrate, there has already been significant distance-building happening inside. Each person, consciously or unconsciously, is beginning to develop more "singleship" than "coupleship." A transition is taking place. Even though a couple may live in the same house, share a sexual relationship and a family, their personal lives are being steered much more toward separate orbits. The marriage itself is becoming an empty house.

Readiness for divorce or singlehood happens when one or both parties have defined themselves quite independently of one another. Being partners is no longer a major source of identity. Identity now comes from the ways they have chosen to be apart.

Sometimes singleness creeps up on a person who is basically unaware that major change has begun. Singleness may not even be a conscious thought. We may even hide it from ourselves. Gradually, though, we begin to feel more comfortable by ourselves, thinking on our own, acting on our behalf, making decisions that exclude our partner and doing things by ourselves that we had once done in our couple world. Now the couple world doesn't seem to fit right. This shift from a twosome to a *onesome* seldom is a simultaneous move by either party, although a divorce often looks, from the outside, as though it were mutually agreed upon from the start. The process of becoming single is usually started by one partner who imagines a far better life with someone else or who has felt pushed to the brink by a relationship that has become too painful to endure.

Figure 2.2. Wall

EMOTIONAL DIVORCE

Before a relationship reaches the point where someone mentions divorce, the couple may already have experienced emotional divorce. Their feelings and behaviors indicate that a definite separation has already happened, even though no one wants to admit it.

An emotional divorce has several warning signs, some fairly obvious and some quite subtle.

Obvious Warning Signs

1. More time is spent with individual friends than with each other.
2. Increasingly more satisfaction is found in work than with each other. Good times with friends and

satisfying work and hobbies are important but excessive attention to these harms relationships.

3. Arguments persist and become more invasive about parents or children. There is an inability to compromise or change behavior.

4. One or both partners are developing a growing dependency on a substance that interferes with health and the ability to feel. These substances include alcohol, drugs, nicotine and food.

5. One or both partners are developing habits that drain energy from the coupleship. These frequently are gambling or excessive TV watching.

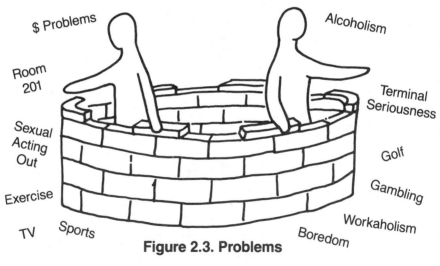

Figure 2.3. Problems

Less specific are the day-to-day changes we tend not to notice until coupleship damage is done:

Subtle Warning Signs

1. Habitual sadness and low energy
2. Boredom and emptiness
3. Indifference to each other's problems and dreams
4. Routine and superficial communication
5. Discomfort with healthy anger
6. Habitual avoidance

7. Decreasing confrontation
8. Sexual coldness and/or avoidance
9. Loss of capacity to play and laugh with each other
10. Frequent feelings of being misunderstood
11. Frequent feelings of loneliness
12. Overbusy and chaotic social or professional life

Even more uncomfortable is the atmosphere of the violence of silence in the home: a chill that sends sparks through every room when the two are together. There is a climate of mutual distrust that can transform the former sanctuary of home into an armed camp. Insults and sarcasm may be common, as well as the loss of small courtesies and politeness.

At this point in the relationship, when no legal steps have yet been taken and whether or not threats of leaving have been made, there may still be a sense that perhaps some magical solution will descend and prevent what seems inevitable. Since each spouse is operating with a different set of ideas and a different set of rules about the relationship, each finds it hard to believe that the other won't *come around* to the "obvious" truth about who's to blame and make behavior alterations that will somehow permit the seriously scarred marriage to survive.

THE DISSATISFIED PARTNER

There comes a point, however, when one partner begins to move toward singleness, almost imperceptibly. Perhaps this person is the more contemplative, more thoughtful spouse. We will call this person the *dissatisfied partner* for the time being. Eventually this person initiates the divorce.

If you identify with this person, you may have spent a great deal of time reflecting and keeping thoughts to yourself. Your concealment is not like lying; it is more like reserving certain thoughts and feelings to yourself for introspection. It is like having a secret place where you can contemplate your situation in private. You may drop the idea of singleness for a while and return to being part of a couple because your thoughts about being single frighten you.

Concern over the apparent approach of singlehood often compels a partner to suggest that maybe the couple should take a vacation. Or go to a counselor. Or sit down to try a different way of talking. The message about the extent of the problem may not be clear to the other spouse. More likely, fear is being manifest as hints. Sometimes there are a number of little side comments that begin as daily complaints. Examples might be:

- "Don't you want to dress up today?"
- "I wish you'd call me when you don't come home."
- "You're not as much fun to be with."

Complaining is an indirect way of saying, "Hey, I'm not really satisfied with us together anymore." Even though it may appear to be negative, it is an indirect attempt to save the relationship, make things as they were originally perceived to be and get involved in the spouse's emotions in a personal way. A positive response to negative remarks may become the only hope that the partner will rejuvenate as a more interesting, attractive and attentive person. Unfortunately, it usually rebounds. Very often the unsatisfactory partner will begin to view the dissatisfied partner as a "bitch," "complainer," "nag" or "criticizer." It's hard for the criticized party to see the positive side of the negative remarks: that the complainer is so desperate to make the spouse attractive again, all subtlety has been abandoned and the likelihood of being negatively perceived has to be risked.

Overt criticism may become a last-ditch effort to try impressing a partner with your dire needs, but there are inherent difficulties in this approach. No one wants to be criticized, challenged or considered wrong. The inevitable lack of response to blunt personal censure only serves to deepen the disappointment of the dissatisfied partner whose reaction must be to pull even further out of the relationship. This person begins to feel more and more isolated, ignored and frustrated. Even if requests for the partner to change have been subtle, dissatisfied partners are disappointed that the spouse hasn't reached out to them. They are cast into an uncomfortable limbo, no longer feeling a part of a coupleship and yet not being single. They can't access the rewards or reinforcement of being a single person but are developing a hunger for validation as an individual now that their identification as part of a team has crumbled. Getting validation becomes very important.

Creating A New Identity

To pursue the security of a new identity, we have to leave our troubled relationships a bit more directly. Generally we try to create a necessary, legitimate absence, such as having to become very, very busy.

I remember at one point in a troubled marriage I became proud that I had three months on my calendar when I was involved in something every single night. I needed the validation that busyness gave me as a person much in demand, wanted and important. Other people may have thought that my life looked crazily overscheduled as I flew from one thing to another, but for me and many others, this level of involvement outside the home is enough for a while to make us feel wanted. Joining more groups or finding more activities with friends promotes validation. Support groups, luncheon dates or friends who frequently go to movies help us prove that we are capable of creating an entirely new social life on our own.

Others simply go back to school. They start taking classes, focus on a new career or aim for a graduate degree. It is not just coincidence that so many people develop an interest in furthering their education later on in life. They might become involved in some kind of self-improvement course, join a fitness center to start running — miles from home. A preoccupation with redesigning their body parallels the change they hope will occur in their personal lives.

Others prefer to become totally lost in parenting. They begin to involve themselves intensely with one or more of their children. The down side of this is that many times they look to a child to be a surrogate spouse. Later on, when the parents are in a position to form responsible adult relationships, these children feel rejected. Too often children are used to fulfill many of the needs of their parents that should be placed elsewhere.

THE FINAL STEPS TO DIVORCE

Some dissatisfied partners simply "drop out." I remember a friend telling me about her husband who later left the relationship. For about six months before he left, he would sit in a rocking chair in front of the stereo listening to the song *To Dream The Impossible Dream.* He talked to no one, didn't share any particular needs or hopes with anyone, and then one Easter Sunday morning, he stood up from his chair, said goodbye to his family and walked out, never to return.

Other variations of escape into near-singlehood are developed by those who become very intensely involved with soap operas, football games or golf. These are solo activities that physically take someone away from a relationship but, even more, isolate a person from emotional contact.

The most overt action to render a relationship impossible is that of taking another lover. Unless heroic efforts are later made to save the marriage, the spouse who decides to have an affair most likely will be the one to leave a coupleship, the person who will be asking for the divorce.

Divorce often is simply the result of seeking validation outside of a marriage in which the desired level of approval has become increasingly unavailable.

Not every dissatisfied spouse sets out to get a divorce. Most of the time the unhappy partner is simply trying to find some relief from aloneness and loneliness in a relationship. As discontented partners begin to collect a positive new identity, they are pulled further and further out of the coupleship. After attempts fail to elicit more positive regard from the partner who will be left, the leaver's need for validation grows larger and larger. The drive to complete the process becomes overwhelming and at that point the "divorce" word surfaces. Frequently the dissatisfied partner becomes so tired of trying to hold up both ends of the relationship with no return that the negatives of divorce no longer outweigh the perceived positives. The end must be signaled, either through direct confrontation ("I'm leaving!") or through intimations by the leaver that the relationship is in really serious trouble and that there's only one solution left: divorce.

TRYING TO MAKE IT WORK — TOO LATE

Sometimes couples belatedly go into a period of time called "trying to make it work." Generally it is the person to be "left behind" who holds the most hope to successfully patch up the marriage. By the time a major crisis in the relationship is underway, the potential leaver has already gone through the intense feeling, thinking and trying processes that the other partner may be just beginning to grapple with. As a result, the dissatisfied spouse probably has concluded there isn't much of a chance. By the time the partner is made aware of the nearness of the marriage's dissolution, it is often too late.

Yet both people may be afraid, for their own futures as well as those of any children involved. "What are my chances of finding anyone better?" "I'm too tired to go back into the dating scene." "The competition is rugged now that I'm older." They may make every possible effort to hang onto the relationship, even though there is no substance left. The known is familiar, despite the fact that it may be awful. An epic effort to make married life "wonderful" may be initiated on the part of the partner who is afraid of being left. Seldom does it feel real, and seldom does it work because, in the real world, the relationship has ended. What worked for them in the beginning no longer exists or was insufficient to carry them through the adversities of married life. The hurts may run too deep.

By this time most couples agree to go into counseling, but with two very different points of view. One person is going in to save the marriage. But often the other is hoping that the counselor will convince their partner that the marriage cannot be salvaged. Usually a counselor can tell quickly whether there is a chance for compromise and healing. Often the best that can be done — and is considerably helpful in view of the hurdles often ahead — is to relieve the tension, validate each party's right to their own special needs and reduce the desire for blaming so they are able to deal more directly with each another.

This late-stage counseling shouldn't be confused with the kind of marriage and family counseling that should have taken place when misery first set in. When counseling is sought as a last resort, as leavers are heading out the door, the time needed for rebuilding a relationship isn't available; leavers usually are anxious to pursue the growing security of the new self-image they have been privately creating. The former sense of security from the marriage is gone. They are fearful of opening old wounds.

Although late-stage counseling may be futile in terms of mending the marriage, it can be valuable to help separating couples communicate honestly, minimizing sarcasm or ridicule. While this directness also can cause hurt and pain in the short run, its focus away from changing and punishing the other person is a valuable aid in resolving the division of a household peacefully.

SHARING THE UNIVERSAL FEELINGS OF DIVORCE

We may not know exactly when a relationship begins to grow apart. Perhaps it began as the result of a single event; maybe it was a slow-growing process formed of several incompatibilities. What we do know is that a growing distance occurs that destroys the bond between two people, and long before the seriousness of the problem is recognized, the dynamics of separation have begun. Despite attempts to "make it work," the marriage falters and one or both of the spouses begins to feel more single than coupled.

The reality of divorce can be shattering and painful and, at the same time, relieving and hopeful. We can all see ourselves somewhere in this book. Although each person's situation is unique, we share certain universal experiences in divorce. It's nice to know none of us is really alone.

There are some very frightened people who refuse to even *think* the "divorce" word. Now that you've read this far, it shows you've got the courage it takes to continue exploring the pros and cons of getting a divorce. Congratulations!

3

The Leaver
And The Left:
Both Hurting,
Both Healing

Joan: I used to keep a lid on my feelings, especially when the children were involved. Sometimes I wanted to complain about Alan's approach to raising kids, which basically was to let them do what they wanted. I wished he would take us to the lake more often, like we did before the kids were born. But whenever I even began to suggest we might do things differently, he would freeze up and have something to do out in the garage.

Then, after months of holding back, I'd blow up over something. It was usually unrelated to our biggest problems. But he'd turn on me and right away I'd get defensive because I knew I was overreacting. In some ways it was a relief to be arguing over a safe topic like his leaving the newspaper all over the house. At least we were talking and letting off some steam. That way we could both fight over things that didn't matter. But things that did matter were off-limits and getting worse.

Ken: When we first got married, we had a ball. After being college sweethearts, it was like we were playing house. We were the beautiful people, even belonging to the Junior League. I started joining clubs and service organizations for good business contacts. She got involved in volunteer work. We went out mostly with other couples, business friends. Then we started having less time on weekends to ourselves. The kids were born, but Amanda got them a nanny and hardly slowed down at all.

She loved shopping and socializing. I was always proud of her looks and popularity. I felt lucky to have a good household manager and a partner who got involved in the community. But she just didn't seem to be very involved with me as time passed. I guess I was too busy establishing myself and paying the bills to give that the importance it deserved. Getting ahead professionally and socially was very important to us. I began to notice after several years that we hardly ever did anything fun, just the two of us. As I found out later, no wonder we didn't, since she had other male "friends" available. At that point I felt I had to end the marriage before everyone found out.

Kathy: I explained to Jim that I liked to keep active. I told him if he wanted, he could join me. What else was there to say? I wasn't going

to quit exercising and feeling good about myself just to sit home and crochet or whatever.
One day I came home from my aerobics class
and there was a note on the kitchen table. All
it said was "Dance away, young lady. I've left."
 I was devastated. He filed for divorce.
There'd been no talking about it and no
advance warning that things were so bad.
He wanted to just throw the marriage away
without even trying to work on it. I was lost.
I didn't know what else to do except go back
to Mom and Dad. I felt I was worth nothing.
And I did nothing — for a year-and-a-half.
It was as if I was a lump with no life.

 Bob: Deena really burned me up. She knew
I was a go-getter, hardly the kind of guy who
sits with his feet propped up, drinking beer in
front of the TV all weekend. That was her
dad, the kind of guy she said she was trying to
avoid marrying. One of the things she liked
most about me before we were married was
how I could go anywhere and do what needed
to be done. But then she started complaining
that I was going and doing too much. How do
you put the brakes on sales and success?
 All I asked was that she come out of herself
a bit to say hello to some nice people once in a
while. But no. Instead, she started drinking
and smoking too much. Then she started to
lose control over our oldest son. He got in
trouble and we had to take him for counseling.
That's when I found out how much trouble
our marriage was really in. And I came to the
conclusion that I wanted out.

Any unraveling relationship will result in a split that inevitably turns one ex-partner into a "leaver" and the other into the "left," each with separate sorrows, guilt, problems and challenges. Certain emotional red flags are hoisted over the home when these critical new roles are about to be assumed. These signs represent levels of deterioration that have been allowed, like rust on a piece of machinery no longer functional, to spread destructively through a relationship. Most often this happens because one or both parties have been unable to talk out critical problems, either by themselves or in counseling.

EIGHT SIGNS OF THE UNRAVELING RELATIONSHIP

Perhaps you recognize these eight stand-off situations from your own experience:

1. Arguments tend to erupt unexpectedly. One partner doesn't even know there is a problem until the other's temper is raging.
2. Negative emotions, especially anger, escalate very quickly.
3. There is a pattern of decision-making that puts self-interest above the interest of the relationship.
4. Fear and anxiety mount when you know you have to talk something over with your partner.
5. Fighting usually develops when one person is attacking and the other is defending.
6. You both know what will start a fight, what it will be like, how it will end and how you will feel. As it begins, there is that "Here we go again" feeling.
7. Your lack of confidence grows in being able to solve a relationship problem.
8. More and more you tend to do fun things together less and less.

BEING THE FIRST TO LEAVE

What can be harder than making the decision to leave a marriage? It involves all our hopes and fears for ourselves (and any children we may have), and often our friends' and relatives' opinions and our relationships with them. It's never a snap decision — although it may be announced quite unexpectedly — but it builds on a series of negative conclusions that become irreversible when our experiences with our partners don't get better. No matter how much we may talk out the pros and cons of leaving with others close to us, usually the cheering section is very small as we take the step to end a marriage. Friends may know the specifics of our discontent, but few people can imagine the level of inner turmoil behind our decision. Broken marriages can be threatening to others who feel a little unsure of their own marriages and many friends also shrink from having to take sides.

Leavers need support systems, too. It's often easier for the "left" party to find sympathy from family and old friends. Often leavers need to find new, caring and understanding people.

The impossibility of fully sharing how hard we tried to save our marriage adds to the guilt, fear and sadness we, as leavers, usually suffer. Added to the despondency of leaving our hopes behind is the fear of being misunderstood, of being judged as selfish and of losing important relationships with people who feel they can be "loyal" only to the left-behind spouse. Leavers often feel that they should have tried harder, should have been willing to change more and should have been willing to stay, even if they were perpetually unhappy. Leavers may realize how preoccupied they've been with unmet needs and feel remorse which hampers their recovery from guilt.

LEAVERS TEND TO GAIN TIME, LOSE SUPPORT

Who was dissatisfied the most? Who made the earliest effort to make the marriage work? Often it's the one we call the leaver. Easily, leavers have some advantages. They have disembarked from the emotional merry-go-round, have made a decision and are no longer expending energy in futile battles and patch-up attempts. They've had time to think through all the positives and negatives of what they are leaving and what they are moving toward. While waiting for the moment when they felt ready to announce their decision, they may even have been able to make advantageous arrangements for finances and a new living situation. Time is on their side. They also have the psychological advantage of being in control of the dissolution of the marriage, rather than perceiving themselves as the "abandoned" ones. If there is any power in the divorce, this person initially may have the greater advantage.

Figure 3.1. The Leaver

Even though the leaver has a sense of power in terms of instigating the divorce, often the one left has unrecognized power within. The power of support from family and friends who rush in to sympathize with the abandoned one can serve as a morale builder which the leaver may not have during the difficult divorce period. The one left can indeed look like "the good guy," a role easily reinforced by friends and family. Although it feels good, such support can actually slow down acceptance and growth in the divorce process.

WHO REALLY WAS THE FIRST "LEAVER"?

The person who has been left has a set of feelings that are actually very similar to the earliest feelings of the leaver: a sense of inadequacy, shame, frustration and anger. The leaver felt these emotions on discovering that the one left couldn't or wouldn't change to suit the leaver's needs. That earlier realization was the point at which the leaver actually felt abandoned or "left" by the spouse who couldn't give what the other expected to get out of the marriage.

So the real difference between "the abandoner" and "the abandoned" is that emotionally the sense of their spouse's leaving them came at different times. The leaver's exit was more overtly expressed, a physical statement paralleling the emotional separation. In actuality, people who are left may have been saying no to the marriage for a long time, but in a more passive way, simply by insisting on being who they were and not being able to conform to the other's very different needs.

Acute pain has the potential of prompting the one left to seek resolutions faster. The leavers often suffer longer while delaying their decisions.

Because the leaver had much more time to think and plan, the divorce may feel much more abrupt for the person who is left. Many people I have talked to felt their surprise, anger, hurt and fear were extremely painful because of this suddenness. Leavers often spend months and years hurting before they finally leave. The ones left are motivated to act fast, make decisions quicker and often feel they must seek professional help to relieve the sudden spiral into acute pain. But their hurting time actually may be shorter because of the shock that motivated them to get this help.

THE ONES LEFT NEED TO MOVE ON

If we are the ones left, we may have daydreamed that the marriage could be magically saved and parting avoided, despite the negative signs. Perhaps the most wrenching feeling when a divorce takes place is that of being left by someone who once desperately wanted to be with us forever and now can't wait to clear out. Whether love was based on just a fantasy that gradually evaporated or whether unforeseen emotional incompatibilities surfaced in crisis, divorce is extremely painful for anyone who clings to the hope that the marriage could have been saved.

Figure 3.2. The Left

The partner who wants the marriage to continue frequently feels trapped and powerless. Often a great deal of conflict continues between the two parties. If the one left does not acknowledge anger toward the leaver for cancelling the marriage, depression (actually the result of anger kept inside) may set in. If we let this type of thinking continue too long, we erode our self-worth. We need to feel our anger, inadequacy and fear but we have to acknowledge them as emotions that will pass. They will become obsolete and we will let them go as we shape a new life.

In addition to being angry, the one left often feels inadequate. "What did I do wrong? Why did I receive this treatment? Am I unlovable?" The period immediately following the event of being left is a critical time for the person surprised by divorce, when it's important to reach out for support and help. Asking for this help is not to be confused with rallying support for ourselves by ex-spouse-bashing.

Outsiders will never know or understand the whole story behind any couple's divorce. Moral support is easier for them to share than anger.

If you feel you have been left, you may need to:

1. *Share feelings with an objective outside party in order to drain off toxic feelings that can harm yourself or others.* This should be a professional person (counselor, clergy, therapy group). Twelve-Step programs are good supports for someone in pain but are not an appropriate place to share and explore the most intense personal feelings.

2. *Obtain good legal advice so that both partners can work out a fair and just divorce settlement.* It is to the advantage of both partners to make a fair settlement and end all emotional and financial ties. With these connections severed, each partner can become more fully single and independent, and heal from the pain of divorce. Too often financial connections keep the pain in progress.

If children are involved, there are critical and important issues surrounding child support. Both parents must assure that the safety and support of their children hold first priority. Many books are devoted entirely to the issues of child support and custody. No divorcing parent has ever regretted the time spent on researching this topic. Many who didn't do this have regretted not learning enough on their own.

Former partners — both the leaver and the one left — who are responsible for themselves only, need to become single, independent people. Among the couples I interviewed, those reporting positive experiences with divorce had ended their financial connections on the day of settlement and divorce finalization.

The old style of ongoing alimony prolongs the self-image or projected image of each divorce partner as still being part of a couple. This financial link also retards the ability of either partner to recover a sense of sufficiency and self-worth.

A RELEASE FROM PAIN

There is pain and possibility for both the leaver and the one left. The challenge is not to become bogged down with who has the greater hurt but to acknowledge and address hurt and hope as stages of growth.

When we have invested ourselves in the life of another and allowed that person to become part of our lives, we may feel as though we are losing a part of ourselves when a divorce takes place. Some spouses have described the sensation as losing a physical component, "a hole in the stomach" feeling. In this vulnerable state we may be convinced that we will never heal. And yet, with time and effort, we do. When we add good support systems and

often professional help to our new lives, the time to heal
becomes less and the effort easier.

By reminding ourselves of the circumstances of the
leaver and the left, we can again reassure ourselves that
both have advantages and disadvantages in a divorce. A
leaver is not someone who simply sits down one day, decides to end a relationship, makes a plan and carries it out.
Leavers are people who are or have been acutely unhappy.
Sometimes in the very beginning they don't even know it
is the relationship they are unhappy with. But they try to
help the relationship. They make an effort to confront the
situation and solve it in their own way. They make many
little choices. In order to protect themselves and to give
their changed sense of not belonging some validation, they
begin to develop some of their singleness. It is only later
that what began as a very subtle restlessness manifests as
the decision to leave a relationship.

On the other hand, spouses who are left behind may
not be aware that they were actually the possessors of a
tremendous amount of power during the relationship.
They had the power to maintain the status quo by not
picking up on the signals of those first motivated to leave,
thereby delaying the divorce process. Possibly the ones
left didn't catch the emotional drift of their partners because they were preoccupied with many things: the home,
children, jobs or excess family baggage.

We keep a healthier perspective if we remind ourselves
that all along in every marriage there are two people, not
one: two people with different ways of handling unhappiness. These two people sometimes begin to drift and become more single. Finally, one of them simply puts a spot-
light on reality and says, "This is no longer working. I'd
like to end the hurt."

With the focus on stopping the pain so that two lives
may seek more positive experiences, we may find that
divorce is a little easier to view objectively. Learning how

differently people express themselves, we see how many divorces are blameless situations in which each partner lets go, acknowledging the other's right to change or not to change, to be as she or he is — *for better or for worse* — regardless of someone else's needs. This is a right we all fought for as toddlers, and even as teens. It is one right we can't expect ourselves or anyone else to forfeit as a maturing adult without enduring an unacceptable level of pain. We release one another from any promises made before we knew what the future held, and we permit ourselves to create a new home with a nourishing atmosphere free of coercion and crippling conflict, where we can grow in peace.

4

Trauma Recovery Begins With Planned Self-Care

Joan: I think Alan's spitefulness over my wanting a divorce affected me a lot at that time, and it's why I gave up so much. I didn't want to be hateful like him. He felt I had misled him and that I wasn't the person I had seemed to be when we first got married. That last part was true: I had changed. I wasn't a playful little dog on a leash and I wasn't a follower anymore. First because he had stopped being the kind of leader I wanted to follow, and then I realized we all need to be our own leaders.

Still, I felt guilty that I got married before I was really ready. Marrying Alan was a way for me to leave a bad family scene. He had been my boss at a summer job during high school. That was when my mother was getting

into pills to escape her situation with my dad.
So I just escaped with Alan.

When we separated, I was too guilty about
leaving him to clarify support for me and
the kids. He never has contributed to their
upbringing. Now I think it's a wonder the court
didn't step in and protect us. I was so foolish
back then.

Ken: Between my wife's affairs and the
divorce, I wasn't looking very good. I tried to
cover up by acting as though I just wanted her
to be happy, as if that's all I ever wanted.
I let her take the car, the house, the place in
the country, the TV, the stereo, the yard
equipment — the whole nine yards! See who
she's leaving? Mr. Good Guy! I gave her the
bulk of my assets. I didn't want her
bad-mouthing me afterwards. And I didn't
want to talk about it in court.

The entire thing was very embarrassing. But
I figured I'd made it once, so I could make it
again. Of course, I was older. But after a while
I realized that I was also a lot lighter. I had
unloaded a lot of illusions and excess baggage,
just dead weight. It took several months, but
my energy level climbed higher than it had
been before we split. Money couldn't buy that.

Kathy: We didn't get involved with lawyers.
We had been renting an apartment and were
together for only two years, so we hadn't
bought much. He took his stuff, I took mine
and that was it. The hard part for me was
facing myself as a failure. I just couldn't figure
out where I had gone wrong. I mean, a lot of

women in my classes were doing just what I
was doing and they weren't divorcing. I laid
around for a long time hating myself, with
little energy to do anything, much less
aerobics.

At some point I finally lost interest in hating
myself. I guess something in me needed to
start moving again. I figured the only thing
I really knew how to do was be myself, but
maybe I could get more involved with others.
I volunteered with kids at a hospice. I had a
chance to do summer theater. I made some
girlfriends, instead of always needing a guy
with me to be with other people. My whole
life wasn't depending on one person to care for
me and it felt good.

Bob: I wanted out and I wanted it over
for good, but this wasn't going to be some
giveaway. She didn't deserve it. But there was
no way we could talk about a settlement without getting angry. I didn't trust her and she
didn't trust me. So we both got lawyers and
spoke through them. That really worked out
for the best. Let them do the squabbling. I'd
had enough. I wanted what was mine and I
wanted it over and done with. No loose ends.

Being in my own place by myself was
strange at first. I bought a bunch of
comedians' records and put them on when I
came home. I took a fat marking pen and
wrote my best qualities in big letters on sheets
of paper and pasted them up in every room so
I couldn't miss them. I also listened to
motivational tapes just to get some upbeat
sounds in my head. And then I spent more

time with my friends my ex-wife didn't like
and introduced my kids to some of my friends'
kids.

A divorce!
We may push the panic button more than once. Bells
and sirens sound. The future may look like an enormous
void, the present like a scramble of cold legal moves and
hot emotions. We may feel alternately numb and then
overwhelmed with countless changes and decisions.

We are anxious to settle everything immediately, to
erase the blackboard of unhappiness so we can put all that
was (and might have been) behind us. We yearn to find a
secure new place for ourselves in the world.

In the midst of all this need of ours — this looking for
peace, support, security and hope — we may distract ourselves from self-care action now. A preoccupation either
with the past and how it could have been different, or
with fears for the future, is natural at this period in our
lives. Too much introspection, however, can become an
energy drain. The person who is filled with rage or
nostalgia and dwells on being victimized becomes tired
through self-neglect. At this place in our lives we need
more energy, not less. We can obtain this vitality through
many positive self-care practices.

*A level head with a positive attitude in a
healthy and strong body is far more receptive to
inspiration and new ideas.*

THE WHOLE PERSON CONCEPT

There has long been a romantic concept that you become "more" when you become part of a couple. In the old
Barbra Streisand song, "People Who Need People," we see
again the strong message: "I was half, now I'm whole."

The corollary is that if I divorce, I become "half" again. All these messages of society affect our emotions when we divorce, but as we recover from the initial trauma of separation, we can see just how negative and misleading these illusions are. One of the reasons couples often run into serious difficulty is that they have looked to the other to provide qualities they have not developed in themselves. A dependence on the spouse results, and when the spouse leaves, or must be left, there's a hole where the sense of being "whole" was.

If we come from a painful family background, we may have a harder time achieving a healthy feeling of wholeness. Our emotions may be tangled up with the classic symptoms of a dysfunctional family past, including:

- Self-denial
- Low self-esteem
- Taking on responsibility for the problems of others
- A low level of self-care

Fortunately, many people who were in difficult situations as youngsters are more able to work through adult stumbling blocks. In therapy they can draw on their history of resiliency and strength. Focusing on the positives of our childhood, in which we were often required to cope on our own, we may recognize that at a very young age, when we had less experience, we were still able to weather a number of daunting storms. Again, focusing on the positive, we can turn our past coping skills into positive tools for living, using them in a healthy way after a divorce.

A device to raise our awareness of these skills is The Whole Person Concept Wheel, shown in Figure 4.1. With it, you can periodically inventory your own personal powers as a reminder to get you going and keep them charged.

OUR SIX POTENTIAL POWERS

When you stare your post-divorce reality in the face, instead of peering at it through a haze of gloom and doom, you might be surprised at the power you have available to yourself, with or without someone else as a partner. Actually we all have six potential areas of power, each well able to reinforce our ability to relate to ourselves, one another, our environment and the world around us. Becoming and remaining aware of these six areas and their interaction helps us keep ourselves in balance. Reminding ourselves of this *whole person concept* can chase off self-doubt in those wavering moments when we're tempted to feel that we are inadequate.

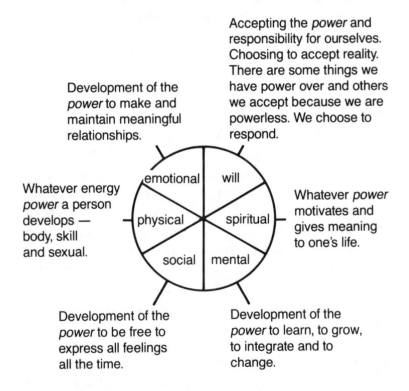

Accepting the *power* and responsibility for ourselves. Choosing to accept reality. There are some things we have power over and others we accept because we are powerless. We choose to respond.

Development of the *power* to make and maintain meaningful relationships.

Whatever energy *power* a person develops — body, skill and sexual.

Whatever *power* motivates and gives meaning to one's life.

Development of the *power* to be free to express all feelings all the time.

Development of the *power* to learn, to grow, to integrate and to change.

Figure 4.1. The Whole Person Concept

Within every person there is a sense of power that is a recognition of the basic fact of our existence. This existence shows ourselves to be what we are. As long as we are physically capable, we are always free to exercise these six powers in expressing ourselves. When we feel robbed of power by circumstances, it is good to get in touch with these essentials:

1. *Our Physical Power* shows itself in our choice to care for and respect our bodies. Issues of diet, exercise and grooming are part of this. Ridding our bodies of nicotine and other harmful substances is an expression we can choose, along with relinquishing workaholism. Our physical power is a valuable source of personal energy. It includes our sexuality: appreciating ourselves as male and female. Making healthy choices as to how to respond to issues of sexuality is an important part of our divorce recovery.

This power has more than just a functional use. It can be employed in enjoyment, such as in sports, music or touch.

2. *Our Mental Power* may be directed toward learning, growing, understanding and integrating knowledge into experience. It has three major subdivisions: memory, vision and fantasy.

Our memory can help us remember the good times. As we heal, it will be increasingly possible to reflect on what we accomplished in this relationship and honor the best parts. This will be important to our sense of self-appreciation.

Vision is what allows us to look ahead and make plans for our future. When we can visualize change and consider all options in our future, we tap into an inner strength and energy that help those changes come about.

Fantasy is the exciting part. It goes a step beyond vision and encourages us to imagine and stretch the possibilities.

Many a fantasy became a dream, then a vision, then a plan and then an actual happening!

All are beneficial in recovery and should be used *for* us, rather than against our new needs. We need to fully use our mental powers in divorce recovery to look at alternatives, see connections and set priorities.

3. *Our Emotional Power* turns us on to the highs and lows, the joys and sorrows, love and hate, cautions and vulnerabilities of life. It is a source of richness. To feel what we feel, name it and talk about it makes our life more understandable, less confusing and less frightening. Our capacity to tune in to feelings opens us up to insight, intuition and reality. There are about 150 feelings we are capable of experiencing, and the more we choose to let them come through, the more energy and insight we will have.

Following is a list of many feelings we can use to help understand ourselves and others:

Abandoned	Challenged	Fascinated
Adamant	Charmed	Fearful
Adequate	Cheated	Frantic
Affectionate	Competitive	Frightened
Agonized	Conspicuous	Frustrated
Angry	Deceitful	Glad
Annoyed	Defeated	Good
Anxious	Delighted	Gratified
Ashamed	Deprived	Greedy
Bad	Discontented	Grieved
Beautiful	Distracted	Grounded
Betrayed	Distraught	Guilty
Bitter	Disturbed	Gullible
Bored	Dubious	Happy
Brave	Eager	Hateful
Burdened	Embarrassed	Helpful
Calm	Empty	Homesick
Capable	Excited	Honored

Hurt	Overwhelmed	Shameful
Ignored	Pained	Silly
Impressed	Peaceful	Skeptical
Infatuated	Persecuted	Sorrowful
Inspired	Pitiful	Talkative
Jealous	Pleasant	Terrified
Joyous	Pretty	Trapped
Lazy	Quarrelsome	Uneasy
Lonely	Queasy	Unsettled
Loving	Raging	Violent
Low	Rejected	Vivacious
Lustful	Relieved	Vulnerable
Mad	Remorseful	Weepy
Miserable	Resentful	Wicked
Nervous	Righteous	Worried
Nutty	Sad	Worthless
Obnoxious	Scared	Zany
Outraged	Self-conscious	Zestful

4. *Our Social Power* is available to affect our relationships with others. When changing a relationship with a significant person in our lives, we can truly appreciate our relationships with all others. We need family, friends and co-workers to help us through this time. It's a period in which we should use our personal power to meet our needs in many ways. This personal power lets us respond to our needs:

- I want . . .
- I need . . .
- I have . . .
- I'll give . . .

Our social power enables us to offer ourselves to others and to build trust. Knowing when to say no and when to say yes gives us power. We learn to be more assertive in asking for our needs to be met, and also when to say no to a relationship or friendship. As we heal, we choose increasingly healthy connections to the people around us. Social power can be used to develop and maintain close, honest relationships in which we love and are loved.

5. *Our Spiritual Power* challenges us to find our own values and the meaning of life — how we fit into this world. This power opens us to all possibilities. Choosing to be open to it unites us with others and becomes a thread of connection. Meditation, prayer and people all become avenues for its expression in our lives. When a major change or trauma occurs in our lives, we are often catapulted into new levels of awareness that include a spiritual dimension. A very wise mentor once said to me, "When you don't know how to go forward, but know you can't go backwards, you can simply stand still and a transformation will begin." Often this leads to a better understanding of one's spirituality.

6. *Our Will Power* is that which decides or doesn't decide, chooses to do or not to do, follows through or changes direction, places values, sticks to decisions and follows through with promises. There is also a subtle side to this power of volition: acceptance. Acceptance, when made as a choice, is part of one's responsibility to oneself.

The *whole person concept* is a growth process, a process of progressively recognizing that you own yourself. It is a way of becoming aware of our own energy and its many facets. It's as if we are becoming the board chairperson in charge of our lives. In this post we would naturally choose as board members only those people who are supportive for us. So it is essential to remember *you* are the board chairperson.

As we grow in the awareness of wholeness, we see more clearly our reality as it is. When we choose to be more fully conscious of who we are now, we know we have a right to be this way. We know what a treasure we are, and we know what parts of ourselves we don't treasure enough. Knowledge gives us the ability to choose change.

DEVELOPING A SENSE OF SELF-WORTH

Another of my books, *Learning to Love Yourself,* talks a great deal about developing a sense of self-worth, the basic ingredient in the motive for self-care. If we take a closer look at the term by dictionary definition, we find *self* means personal, having its own identity and personality. *Worth* is about deserving value and being useful. My own version of the definition is:

🍀

Self-worth: *My valuable identity, deserving all good things.*

High self-worth says, "I want to feel high energy and a sense of freedom. I want to know and care about myself." When we're connected with a sense of high self-worth, it means that we are able to . . .

- *Make choices that affect the way we live.* We are not helpless creatures drifting passively at the mercy of the winds of chance and on the currents of someone else's fortune. We have choices and can actively determine our own existence.
- *Enjoy our own bodies.* We are multidimensional beings — mentally, spiritually, emotionally and physically. We can take equal pleasure in all of these dimensions.
- *Recognize and accept that the way we feel about ourselves inside affects the way we relate to people out in the world.* When we feel positive about ourselves, we are able to build and maintain positive, life-enhancing relationships, and we are able to relate to people in meaningful and satisfying ways.
- *Truly experience life* as we have the capacity to live it. We know that as we raise our own self-worth, we will feel more integrity, honesty, compassion, energy and love.

All growth depends on a favorable climate, nurturance and a nonhostile environment. Even a tree as big and magnificent as a sequoia can be stunted by harsh environmental conditions. The emotional climate around us is just as influential on our ability to thrive.

Letting relationships just happen to you — rather than purposefully inviting people into your life — is giving up personal power. Surround yourself with those who will support your journey, not detour your needs.

You want people around you who are a comfort to you and will help you build strength and confidence. You do not need increased trauma or criticism.

Figure 4.2. Self-Worth Is About Appreciating Myself

SELF-WORTH PRESCRIPTIONS

Our self-worth continues to increase as we find our lives becoming increasingly manageable. We *make* it manageable. Life begins to work for us because of the *choices* we make.

Following are two prescriptions for us and others. One is to enhance our image of ourselves in our own eyes. The next is to help others feel better about themselves through our actions.

Rx For Self

1. *Accept yourself.*
2. *Trust yourself and others.*
3. *Set realistic expectations.*
4. *Take risks.*
5. *Forgive yourself and others.*
6. *Express your feelings.*
7. *Appreciate your body.*
8. *Be respectful of your ideas.*
9. *Take responsibility for your actions.*
10. *Affirm your values.*
11. *Develop new skills.*
12. *Celebrate your freedom.*

Rx For Others

1. *Let others know you're listening.*
2. *Respect other people's right to an opinion.*
3. *Celebrate other people's achievements.*
4. *Don't let others guess at your expectations; be clear and reasonable.*
5. *Enforce rules and guidelines fairly.*
6. *Appreciate other people's differences.*
7. *Negotiate conflicts; don't make demands.*
8. *Demonstrate your trustworthiness.*
9. *Build confidence by affirming what you want and who you are with others.*
10. *Encourage other people's independence.*
11. *Help others with their struggles.*
12. *Recognize other people's competence.*

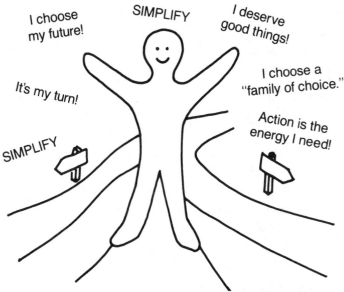

Figure 4.3. I Can Make Choices For Myself
Our self-worth continues to increase as we find our lives becoming increasingly manageable. The manageability of our lives is in direct connection with the choices we make.

BEING SAVVY ABOUT LEGAL MOVES ISN'T BEING MERCENARY

Parallel with your need to take charge of your emotional health should be a sound interest in the financial aspects of dissolving your partnership with your ex-spouse. So many times a divorcing spouse will become only minimally involved in the legal aspects of the separation, either out of disgust, guilt or a lack of awareness of the importance of being informed. However, most people who took this attitude lived to regret it, not realizing the long-term complications and consequences.

Begin legal self-care with the careful selection of an attorney, one of the single most important decisions that you will make about your future. Find this person through trusted sources: referral by your county bar association or another's recommendation. Switch lawyers if you don't feel comfortable with your first choice.

Like a partner in a business, a partner in a marriage needs to be well-represented when the relationship is ending. Don't let strong emotions jeopardize your future; work toward a fair settlement with a competent attorney.

Everyone's settlement is different, according to circumstances, but your goal should be to end the bond in every way possible, so each party is free to move on without ties. When children are involved, both partners need to commit to their care and well-being.

LEGAL GUIDELINES

Some guidelines you won't regret following are:

1. *Freeze all assets for everyone* until the divorce is over. Keep only enough for day-to-day living.
2. *Avoid the do-it-yourself divorce* unless there are no assets and no need for child support.
3. *Don't let one attorney represent both parties.* It seldom works out.
4. *Don't talk directly with your spouse's attorney.* Counsels should talk to each other; you talk only with *your* attorney who is paid to represent your best interests.
5. *Seek firm understanding and good rapport.* If you feel as if you are being asked to do work your attorney is paid to do, speak up. If you feel as if you are chasing your attorney too often and unresponsiveness becomes the rule, question the delays.
6. *Never lie to your attorney.*
7. *Act on your attorney's advice.* Get what you are paying for.

8. *Don't sign any papers or make any agreements without legal counsel.*

9. *Let your lawyer speak for you in legal matters.* If you are inclined to try old manipulative techniques to gain an edge, don't. They may backfire. Unresolved emotions get in the way of making sound legal decisions.

10. *Don't take legal advice from friends.* Every situation is unique. Therefore, you can't safely assume what someone else did will work for you. Laws differ from state to state.

11. *Remember that you are the employer and the lawyer works for you.* Take responsibility for having a plan, knowing what you want and don't want.

12. *Follow through.* Do not assume that things will work out by themselves. Pay attention to action. Know what you need to keep track of and do it. Keep your power.

SELF-CARE STRATEGIES THAT WORK

During the months of loss adjustment, it is beneficial to take the time to focus on self-nurturing, beginning with . . .

Self-Care Move No. 1: *Enjoy the moment.* Instead of wondering how others are going to react and worrying about what people expect of you, center on what you're doing that's right *for you.* Compliment yourself on the matters you handle well; don't let them slide as insignificant. The more you respond to your own needs, the better you will start to feel and the more positively others will respond to you.

Try to set aside at least one hour per weekday and three to four hours each weekend to do just what *you* want to do, frivolous or important. Don't do chores. See a movie, watch a fire in a fireplace, read a book, take a painting class, go antique shopping or go to dinner with friends, but make sure it's what you want to do. This is part of what is called being *proactive* in your own self-care. You are not waiting for someone else to dress up your life or to serve as its centerpiece. By starting to be creative, you will energize yourself with the results, giving you even more power to rework your life.

Self-Care Move No. 2: *Make a pledge that you are going to be more assertive.* So much of people's lives, especially during times of trauma, is involved in trying to win approval from other people. However, being self-sacrificing will not help you heal and will not make you happy. Avoiding anticipated external conflict in this way will only result in inner conflict that is just as painful.

Recognize the parts of yourself that are unfulfilled and realize that this is the time of all times to be positive about yourself and assertive about your right to your own life.

Self-Care Move No. 3: *Focus on your own needs.* There is a technique that helps many people respond less automatically to requests by others which may conflict with their own needs and desires. It is to pause before responding to any request by children, relatives, friends or employers. If you have programmed yourself almost always to be "the good guy," the habit of saying yes when you'd rather say no takes a while to break. Instead, try a standard response such as "I need time to think it over" or "I'll have to check my calendar and get back to you." Then take plenty of time to see if you would say yes because you want to or because someone else wants you to. Make sure the choice is yours. It is very empowering to learn to say no. It will make your yes more meaningful.

Self-Care Move No. 4: *Pay attention to financial developments.* Decide to take a financial planning seminar or join an investment club. You need to go only once every week or so, but if you've never been involved in financial planning, it may open up several new horizons. Many said that learning to handle their finances successfully was a major accomplishment following their divorces.

Also, do one financial favor for yourself. Buy a Certificate of Deposit (CD), look into a mutual fund, buy some
stock and learn how to read the stock report. Each one of
these little ventures on your own will reinforce your power to act and will help you feel better about yourself.

Self-Care Move No. 5: *Guard your privacy.* Don't flee
from it; treasure it! Following a divorce many people an-
ticipate intense suffering from "loneliness," a negative
word that should be turned into a positive like "privacy"
or "aloneness." *Aloneness* is not the same as *loneliness.* Loneliness is concentrating on who you don't have with you to
fill free time. Aloneness is emphasizing the time you have
to do anything you want to make yourself feel happy,
useful, fulfilled, educated, creative, capable, a part of your
community, a positive part of your world, or whatever
else you'd like to do to stretch your mental or physical
being. Your free time is as valuable as anyone else's. Don't
downgrade it because it isn't crowded with demands. Use
it to write the letters you've been meaning to write or
take the naps you always felt would be self-indulgent.
Walk to "nowhere" and back, enjoying every moment and
enjoying your "self."

Self-Care Move No. 6: *Develop a selection of regular "alone"
pleasures.* These could be . . .

1. A special ritual such as reading the newspaper or
   watching the news with your favorite, or a new, tea
   or coffee drink.
2. Getting totally involved in the needs of someone you
   don't know for two hours a week as a volunteer.
3. Indulging in your favorite dishes at a nice restaurant
   for breakfast, lunch or dinner once a week. Find
   some restaurants where you will feel comfortable
   reading a book. Savor going out, having a great meal
   and enjoying the companionship of a good writer
   (and yourself!) all at the same time!

READER/CUSTOMER CARE SURVEY

If you are enjoying this book, please help us serve you better and meet your changing needs by taking a few minutes to complete this survey. Please fold it & drop it in the mail.

Name: _____

Address: _____

_____

Tel. # _____

As a special **"Thank You"** we'll send you exciting news about interesting books and a valuable Gift Certificate.
It's Our Pleasure to Serve You!

(1) Gender: 1) ____ Female 2) ____ Male

(2) Age:
1) ____ 18-25   4) ____ 46-55
2) ____ 26-35   5) ____ 56-65
3) ____ 36-45   6) ____ 65+

(3) Marital status:
1) ____ Married 3) ____ Single 5) ____ Widowed
2) ____ Divorced 4) ____ Partner

(4) Is this book:
1) ____ Purchased for self?
2) ____ Purchased for others?
3) ____ Received as gift?

(5) How did you find out about this book?
1) ____ Catalog   2) ____ Store Display
Newspaper
3) ____ Best Seller List
4) ____ Article/Book Review
5) ____ Advertisement
Magazine
6) ____ Feature Article
7) ____ Book Review
8) ____ Advertisement
9) ____ Word of Mouth
A) ____ T.V./Talk Show (Specify) _____
B) ____ Radio/Talk Show (Specify) _____
C) ____ Professional Referral _____
D) ____ Other (Specify) _____

Which Health Communications book are you currently reading? _____

(6) What subject areas do you enjoy reading most? (Rank in order of enjoyment)
1) ____ Women's Issues/   5) ____ New Age/
         Relationships   Altern. Healing
2) ____ Business Self Help 6) ____ Aging
3) ____ Soul/Spirituality/   7) ____ Parenting
         Inspiration   8) ____ Diet/Nutrition/
4) ____ Recovery   Exercise/Health

(14) What do you look for when choosing a personal growth book?
(Rank in order of importance)
1) ____ Subject   3) ____ Author
2) ____ Title   4) ____ Price
      Cover Design   5) ____ In Store Location

(19) When do you buy books?
(Rank in order of importance)
1) ____ Christmas
2) ____ Valentine's Day
3) ____ Birthday
4) ____ Mother's Day
5) ____ Other (Specify _____

(23) Where do you buy your books?
(Rank in order of frequency of purchases)
1) ____ Bookstore   6) ____ Gift Store
2) ____ Price Club   7) ____ Book Club
3) ____ Department Store 8) ____ Mail Order
4) ____ Supermarket/   9) ____ T.V. Shopping
         Drug Store   A) ____ Airport
5) ____ Health Food Store

Additional comments you would like to make to help us serve you better.

_____

_____

Thank You ¡¡

BUSINESS REPLY MAIL
FIRST CLASS MAIL PERMIT NO 45 DEERFIELD BEACH, FL

POSTAGE WILL BE PAID BY ADDRESSEE

HEALTH COMMUNICATIONS
3201 SW 15TH STREET
DEERFIELD BEACH, FL 33442-9875

4. Exercise — walk, run, swim, bike. You will feel so much better.

ADULT CHILDREN OF DIVORCE
NEED SPECIAL SELF-CARE

If you came from a family in which divorce happened, you should watch for the telltale signs of stress reaction after your own separation. You need to be extra aware of what you are doing, when you do it and why. Children of divorce are often neglected. When they are too young to understand that neglect is not right, children may unconsciously learn and record patterns of neglect as normal and still respond to them as adults. Without realizing that another reaction is more appropriate, you may become self-neglecting after your own divorce.

For adult children of divorce, learning to take care of yourself may be very hard to do. Practice will take you from discomfort to comfort without feeling guilty.

WHEN CARETAKING BECOMES
SELF-ABUSE

By needing to help too much — and by helping the wrong people too often — adult children from painful families can set themselves up for abusive one-way relationships. These caretakers have a low sense of self-esteem that may cause them to think they have to settle for manipulators in their lives: addicts, abusers, alcoholics, workaholics or neglectful friends, children or partners. But when caretakers decide to change, they become more aware of how they let people treat them. Do they want to continue to permit friends and relatives to take advantage of them, misuse their company, criticize their lives or choices, put them in a position they don't want to be in?

Very often family members will try to make divorcing parents feel guilty by dumping their anger on them, rather than taking responsibility for their own feelings. This can become a painful burden to carry.

Sometimes a change in behavior — a refusal to continue being a victim of exploitation regardless of another's apparent need — begins with a simple evaluation of your own needs. Do I need to continue in so much discomfort and pain at this point in my life? Can I survive the trauma of divorce by carrying this additional destructive baggage? The temptation to give in to the old way of holding on to companionship will remain for some time because . . .

- It is familiar.
- It has become automatic.
- It is easy.
- It feels like part of us.

Choosing to be exploited is like the compulsion to do anything else we know isn't good for us: It feels nice for a little while but bad for very much longer.

It is critical for people who have been overly responsible as children, and have taken this behavior into adulthood, to find relationships at this time that are mutually nurturing and supportive. We all need to associate only with people who respect us. We need to learn to identify with our own needs and surround ourselves with people who support — not work against — what we are trying to achieve in our new experience of being on our own.

You cannot be on someone else's "own" and be on your own too. People who want to force their ways on you are counterproductive in divorce recovery.

WHEN SELF-CARE BECOMES SELF-ABUSE

Some of us have grown up in homes where we had to take care of ourselves too much. That became the norm, the main way things happened. Often we were required to reach beyond our grasp, and we "made do" with the results. Whether the outcome was satisfactory or unsatisfactory, we may have turned our unhappiness into a pride that we could do it ourselves. Pride is a good feeling, but too much pride is counterproductive.

In times of adult crisis, such as divorce recovery, we may find that we'd like to bend our tendency to handle every situation by ourselves. We may want to ask for emotional or practical help but are afraid that it could come with strings. Maybe accepting help would feel uncomfortable or threaten our valued sense of independence and control.

Sometimes breaking the patterns of our response to difficulties can open a new, much more comfortable world for us. Human beings are social beings, not isolated organisms. Reaching out for emotional or practical support, from someone who has not misused us in the past, is healthy. Sufficient help may not have been accessible to us as dependent children, but it is readily available in many forms, including professional counseling, now that we are adults. Taking advantage of available support not only puts us in a position to do better faster, but gives those who like to help a chance to feel good.

Healthy behavior can feel unhealthy at first because it is not our norm. Giving and receiving help are both part of healthy living and mutually rewarding.

21 HEALING HELPERS

You may be surprised by how many ideas are available as quick pick-me-ups, ideal for the recently divorced. That's because we who have been through it have had plenty of time to find out what works. So while you're working on deep issues that will take a little time to sort out, here are 21 quick *healing helpers* to offset periodic blues:

1. *Swamped with nostalgia?* Instead of sobbing *too much* over the wonderful times in the beginning and how they went away, turn the emphasis around. Remember how wonderful *you* were in the beginning — approachable, lovable and desirable — and how *you* made the great times happen as much as anyone else.

2. *Feeling unappreciated?* Compliment yourself every day. Maybe your hair turned out great. Or you got a report in on time at the office. Maybe you made that sale. Be generous with self-praise.

3. *Suspect you're not good company?* Negative people are not enjoyable to be around. A simple way to be sought after is to be aware of other people. Give them genuine compliments. Look for things to like and people will like to be with you.

4. *Can't imagine your life ahead?* Creative imaging takes time and practice. Give yourself plenty of time to just daydream and try on possibilities. Like a good sauce that needs time to simmer, daydreams can fulfill your heart's desire in time. Let your thoughts roam; you don't have to plan the rest of your life immediately.

5. *Wish you could get what you want?* Start asking. When a new relationship materializes, speak of your needs. Although awkward at first, speaking up gradually becomes very easy. You can begin with something as small as requesting the TV remote. Don't always let someone else make the choices. Even those who like to be in charge appreciate a break. *You* choose the movie. *You* pick the restaurant more often. Let people know who you are by what you want.

6. *Feel as if you're just marking time?* Decide to grow a bit. Learn something new. Would you like to play a keyboard? Do you really wish you knew computers? Don't most of us want to be able to speak a little Spanish or French when traveling? Would you like to go to a sneak-preview movie? All of these activities are things you can do by yourself. And they will all give you a sense of mastery over your environment.

7. *Swamped with the mundane?* Learn the principles of "delegate or ignore." Don't define yourself by how much you can endure. Whether doing dishes, cleaning house, grocery shopping, doing your taxes or arranging reservations for a trip, do what you want to do, then delegate. If it's not important enough for you to do or to delegate, don't add it to your list of woes.

8. *Not laughing enough?* Listen to comedy tapes. Clip some cartoons and hang them where you'll be reminded you can still laugh. If you can't think of anything funny to say, share a cartoon with someone. Try not looking with a microscope at what went wrong in your day. Imagine you are boarding a plane and then looking down on your day 30,000 feet. A change in perspective can make molehills of mountains, at least long enough to chuckle at some of the things we see in a one-sided way.

9. *Running out of options?* There are always going to be problems in life beyond our control and yet, many things are controllable. Even when they aren't, we still have a choice in how we handle them. When are we going to let something become really big? When are we going to address a problem? When are we going to take action?

10. *Can't think positively?* All of us have the option to think positively but it may not feel right to deny our negative feelings. So have your cake and eat it, too. If you want to say "I'm too fat," follow the negative with "but

I'm starting to exercise" or "I didn't overeat as much as I could have." If you feel "My money's running out," don't pass up the chance to add, "but every single day I'm looking for an opportunity to make more" or "but I'm working on how to manage it better." Celebrate the choices you're making and the critic inside will lose its power as the only influence over your emotions.

Affirm what is going right in your life every day, as well as your role in making good things happen. Don't give up your power to a negative pattern of thinking.

11. You feel like a lump? Make exercise fun and social. Walk in malls. Join a spa. Hike. Get a trainer. As you feel good about yourself physically, you will feel better emotionally.

12. Racing against time? Give yourself a minimum of a year to restore balance, hope and positive feelings. You will need to experience each milestone (Thanksgiving, Christmas, Hanukkah, Valentine's Day, Easter, Fourth of July, birthdays, anniversaries) before the grief cycle is completed and the relief of emotional healing sets in. *Time will heal.*

13. Life too hectic? You may need to create quiet time to reflect, meditate, read . . . an interval to fill with meaning.

14. Need support? Contact with understanding people is easily available in support groups, counseling, therapy or 12-Step groups.

Always remember that asking for help is a sign of strength, not weakness.

Seek both people with similar problems and those without present difficulties. Each group has something to give what you need.

15. *You can't live in the present?* A sane starting point in divorce recovery is to see things as they are rather than the way they were or as we wish they would be.

🌹

If we want to grab hold of a better future, we must let go of the past. Newness needs a space made for it.

---

16. *You're intimidated by your kids?* You can expect them not to understand an adult's decision but don't feel guilty that kids may pout as a result. Shift the focus to what they *can* understand: You love them and they will always be taken care of.

17. *You doubt you can be two parents in one?* It is easy for single parents to become prisoners of their children by trying to overcompensate in every area. Trying to be two people results only in one tired parent. Substitute guilt with more love, not more activity.

18. *Do you miss belonging?* Develop a family-of-choice, an emotional safety net. There are many ways to find supportive people in groups you join. If you don't know how to find them, check with your local newspaper to see what day they print notices of support group meetings.

19. *You can't forgive?* There are many paths to forgiveness, some very effective ones begin with an understanding of ourselves. Ultimately, when we are able to let go and see a better life ahead, we can let forgiveness become a spiritual experience rather than a thought process.

20. *You're afraid to remarry?* Statistics indicate that the majority of all divorced people remarry, despite reservations after their first marriages fell apart. Most people, in time, realize that they are more capable of healthy

commitment because of the insights they've gained through the divorce experience. They may meet resistance to the idea of remarriage from relatives or friends, losing some relationships and gaining others. It's sometimes "win a few, lose a few," but the best way to move into a new marriage is to expect bumps that will be smoothed out a day at a time.

21. *"What ifs" troubling you?* We all make mistakes in marriage but at some point you may realize that this old saying isn't just a cliche: *You are human, too.* Making the decision to let go of the "why" questions, the blame and the guilt, will free you to emphasize your strong points and learn from your weaknesses, not dwell on them. Knowing you have a good heart, send it confidently out into the world and watch it confirm what a good person you are.

5

Feelings Need To Be Felt

Joan: I was feeling sad, missing what I didn't have, and I was lonely. After the divorce, I felt vulnerable. I needed people, as much support as I could get. I went into therapy because I had been overeating and gaining weight due to my depression. I joined a support group of divorced people and a weight control group and made some friends I could talk to. Some of them were women and one was a man.

Maybe I was taking a shortcut out of unhappiness, but I married Doyle. Even if it was a shortcut, I felt more able to take chances and less in need of a fatherly husband. Still, it was a bit much to handle, still recovering from one marriage while taking on a new one. But, my therapist was there for me, regardless of what I decided to do, and so were my new friends.

Ken: For some time after the divorce, I was numb. Thinking about the whole thing just hurt too much, so I started drinking too much, which, of course, just prolonged the agony. I felt nothing was changing, except for my new drinking problem. I had to get better, so I made a strong commitment to an AA group. I lost a lot of self-pity there.

I began having social breakfasts and became involved in other people's lives. I was feeling really ineffectual with my own kids so I decided to get active in some adolescent programs, working with disadvantaged youngsters. That was an upper. Then I figured I might as well stop smoking, as long as I was starting a new phase of my life. I started playing golf for some exercise and went swimming regularly at the "Y." After a while, instead of seeing a bleary-eyed guy in my mirror, I started to look pretty good.

Kathy: I was a zombie for the longest time. I thought my depression would never end. My mother had to take care of me almost like a child for a year 'cause I really wasn't interested in doing anything. Thinking just made it worse. I'd trashed my marriage and that was it.

As I came out of it, I started having mood swings. One day I'd feel I was young enough to get another guy, have a career and make it on my own. Then I'd have a lot of energy and go out running But the next day I'd crash, wonder what I had that anyone would want, and get really depressed about not being able to hold on to Jim, how great I had thought he was, how beautiful the wedding was, how blind I was and so on.

In counseling I got a better perspective on myself. I had been afraid of feeling regrets for the rest of my life. I saw I had really limited ideas about myself and what I could do. After a while I got up the courage to experiment with my life and try some new things.

Bob: Spending more time with my business buddies and other friends, I began to find out that maybe they weren't a great influence on my kids or even on me. I decided to take my teenage son fishing in a new boat we'd shopped for together. He looked forward to these times and so did I. My daughter seemed to lean on her mother more but I was there for her, too.

Then I did some things for myself. I dated. I stopped drinking entirely and two years into the divorce, I was able to stop smoking. Things were rolling again, and better, without the constant conflict. I'd recommend to anyone in my spot to put *The Serenity Prayer* in his wallet. It's realistic and it helped.

HEALING THROUGH GRIEF

Shortcuts don't work with grief.

The only way to heal as quickly and as thoroughly as possible from the wrenching grief of divorce is to walk right through the center of it. You can't go over it, under it or around it without having it come back to haunt you. Why not? Because those feelings are *you*, and you can't escape yourself.

If we try to bury our pain with work or fog it with alcohol or food, recovery is going to take even longer.

Those who do not allow themselves grieving time just put off the process. Later on in life the pain will boomerang, returning to hit us as a neurosis, a compulsion or some other kind of self-defeating behavior. At that point we will have double the work to put our lives back on track.

We need to take the time to examine all the emotions that are affecting us, try to trace them to their source, see how and why the relationship went wrong and then adjust our minds and hearts to the new view of ourselves and our former spouse that will emerge. Grief is part of gaining a new perspective on what was real in our lives — past and present — and what was fantasy. What we grieve over may gradually change in the long re-examination process that is part of the recovery period.

How long will it take? Some people take longer than others, depending on whether they were the leaver or the one left, whether the decision to divorce came suddenly or was brewing for some time, and depending on the nature of the individual.

Fortunately pain like this doesn't come often in most lives, but this makes it even more unfamiliar and uncomfortable. We want the pain to stop but it is in our best interests to learn its lessons, rather than to try to anesthetize it.

We need to recognize that following divorce, life isn't going to be easy for some time. We need to recognize that it is okay to be frightened of the challenges ahead. It's okay to mourn that the dream we once loved to dream is over. Grief is natural and must be allowed. As we reach out for help and go ahead to do what needs to be done, we will still have times of mourning. These periods of pain continue to teach us about the experience we have been through until we don't need them anymore.

Healing from the grief of divorce will happen. As with other hurts, we heal best and most completely if we let all of our feelings drain from the "wound."

PSYCHIC NUMBING

Sometimes when we experience a loss that's great, profound and quick, we become, for a short period of time, incapable of feeling. This is called *psychic numbing*. It can happen when someone dies very suddenly or when several people are wiped out by a tragedy. It is very common among women who find out their husbands are having affairs. Frequently it occurs to the one left when the leaver announces it's time to go.

This anesthetized condition of our feelings is a protection against overwhelming and destructive emotions. Feelings are allowed to surface in a very diffused way or only a few at a time. Sometimes a person will admit, "I don't feel anything . . . I feel numb." But slowly and surely this natural psychic anesthetic wears off and the feeling capacity returns. When this happens, we may be very confused or even panicky. In the end, however, a balance will be created. We will be able to handle our emotions and they will return only in manageable amounts.

AWAKENING FEELINGS

Allowing yourself to feel all feelings that arise is the best way to remain in the healing process. Don't pull a defensive sheet over them, hoping they will go to sleep. If you want them out and away, the only window for them to escape through is your awareness. A big feeling can't squeeze out a pinpoint of awareness. Admit the size of the feeling so you can give it the amount of attention it deserves. Only then will you be dealing with it realistically.

Trying to ignore or bury a strong feeling is sure to fail if your goal is maximum emotional recovery.

Some of the feelings ex-spouses most often reported in my survey were:

guilt	anger	embarrassment
shame	loneliness	depression
fear	sadness	

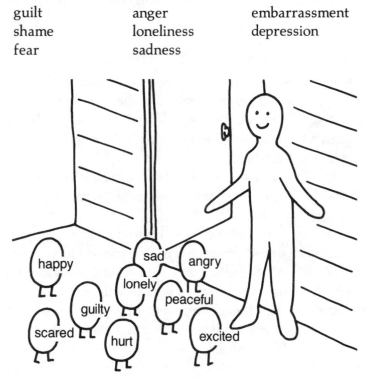

**Figure 5.1. When I Claim All My Feelings,
I Will Know Me . . .**

It's not only the "down" feelings you want to acknowledge but the "up" emotions, too, which may include:

strength	peacefulness	secureness
courage	self-compassion	excitement
responsiveness	confidence	hopefulness

Because the "down" feelings are giving us so much trouble, they tend to crowd the positive emotions off the stage of our attention. But we need to remember that when we

experience our healing emotions, they should not be de-
valued because they don't seem to fit in with our prevail-
ing gloomy mood. To the contrary, positive emotions
should be given star billing as reminders that we have
much going for us under all our temporary turmoil.

CHARTING OUR DAILY MOODS

All of our feelings are on a continuum. They range
from . . .

Pain   Comfort   Joy

Most days our feelings stay in the comfortable range.
Deep pain or euphoric happiness are at either end of the
spectrum. The process of divorce causes an upset among
our "average" feelings and we are bounced every which
way. This is normal and to be expected. One day we're
up; another we're down. What's important is that we accept ourselves, wherever we are, from day to day.

We can see our own hope in the lives of others.
Most of the tremulous feelings experienced by ex-
spouses level out within a year after their divorces.

AVOID MEDICATING YOUR FEELINGS

Feelings will heal only as they are expressed. So it is
important to avoid medicating and running from these
feelings. The temptation is certainly there, most frequently in the form of . . .

alcohol   nicotine
drugs   sugar

Often behaviors are used to achieve the same numbing
effect, and we find people getting involved with . . .

excess eating   *excess* spending
excess work   *excess* sports and/or exercise
excess busyness   *rebounding* into relationships

> *You cannot heal what you cannot feel. You cannot feel what you medicate.*

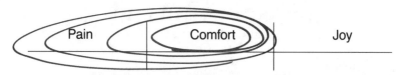

First Year Following Divorce = Emotional Chaos

Eventual Resolution

Figure 5.2. Resolution Of Post-Divorce Feelings

SAFE PEOPLE AND PLACES

We all benefit from sharing our feelings, but it helps to be discriminating about the people we go to with our emotions. The best choices are:

Counselors

Support groups

Selected friends

Selected family

Characteristics of safe people include these descriptions:

They do not ridicule.

They do not belittle.

They are not sarcastic.

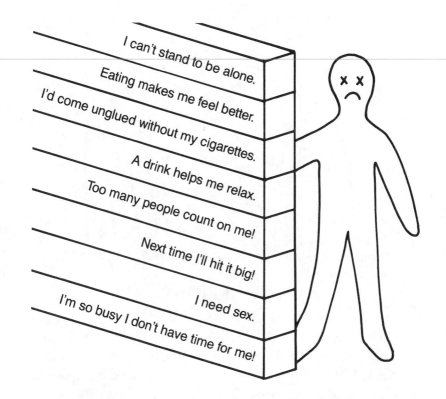

I can't stand to be alone.

Eating makes me feel better.

I'd come unglued without my cigarettes.

A drink helps me relax.

Too many people count on me!

Next time I'll hit it big!

I need sex.

I'm so busy I don't have time for me!

Figure 5.3. Avoid These Ways To Medicate Feelings

Be careful not to share everywhere or all the time. Divorce is a process you are going through. It is not the core of your identity or lifestyle. You are more than your identity as a divorced person. As compelling an issue as it is to you now, focusing only on this with family members and friends can be detrimental to your own self-image and your relationships. Don't expect others to feel the degree of your hottest emotions. Don't burden them with your expectations of an emotional response equal to yours. Blame is something we learn to work out best within ourselves or with professional support as we grow in understanding of our marriage experience.

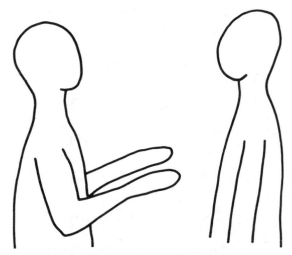

Figure 5.4. Safe People And Places Are Important

DIVORCE CEREMONY MAY
AID IN CLOSURE

One problem in divorce recovery is the lack of closure to the experience. Unlike any other loss of a person, there is no dignified ceremony to mark the end of one experience and the beginning of another. Attending a memorial service after a death, saying goodbye to your classmates at graduation, watching a father "give away" his daughter — all of these occasions publicly acknowledge our sadness at an ending as well as our hope for a new beginning.

If I had my way, I would have divorce ceremonies preceded by divorce announcements, with people coming together to give support and acknowledgment, helping each person make the transition. There would be no shame or blame. We need to have the option of an open statement of divorce in order to commemorate the fact that there has been a "death" or ending. This important loss deserves a dignified and blameless acknowledgment acted out in ceremony or, at least, documented in some human and social way, not just legally.

We need to incorporate this important milestone into our lives as we each go our separate ways. A formal good-bye to the marriage would emphasize its finality and help boost us out of the past and into the present. By the time we are ready to divorce, everyone knows the negatives and what the pain was like. Focusing on what was good and the importance of letting go of the pain, we could support one another in a much more positive singleness. Probably one of the greatest benefits of a formal divorce would be for the children. They would see their parents being able to part in a dignified ritual, and that the relationship responsible for bringing them into this world was dissolved with respect for its importance to them.

Following is a sample divorce ceremony which includes many blame-eliminating statements and acknowledges mutual responsibility for the ending of the relationship, as well as mutual goodwill for the future. It closes with a request for forgiveness and the Serenity Prayer.

ᕉOur Divorce CeremonyᕉҚ

On this day we come together, with some sadness, to accept that our marriage is dissolved.

On _____ (date) in _____ (city and state), we were married. We thought on that day that we were entering a marriage that would be permanent. We had plans, hopes and fears.

What we didn't know and didn't plan on is the fact that we had each come to the marriage with parts of ourselves unknown. These unknowns prevented us from seeing ourselves clearly and also kept us from getting to know one another. As we have grown and changed, we have not been able to grow together. It has become clear that we cannot go on as a couple any longer.

We have tried to give each other love, comfort and support. We did not set out to hurt one another. Guilt, fear, shame and hurt have become a part of our life. There have been many misunderstandings, and at times each of us felt the other was responsible for what was happening. We did not realize that both of us brought pain to the relationship.

Inside each of us were two wounded and frightened children who needed support and healing. Neither of us has been able to give what was needed and perhaps neither of us was able to receive what was needed. We did our best over the years.

After _____ _(# of years)_, we admit defeat. We are not defeated as two individuals; we are simply defeated in making this union work.

We have made a decision to obtain a divorce. Each of us will find our own way to heal. We will cope and lend support to each other as we go our separate ways.

Even though we could not fulfill our plans as a couple, our prayer is that we will fulfill our separate lives in our own way.

We ask forgiveness of each other. We have each forgiven ourselves and ask that our families, our community and our God support our decision.

THE SERENITY PRAYER

God grant me the serenity to accept the things I cannot change,
the courage to change the things I can, and the wisdom to know the difference.

— Parts of this ceremony were written by
Virginia Lisenbee Davis

6

Losses Make Lasting Lessons

Joan: I carried a big burden of guilt for about ten years after my divorce. It ruled decisions I made for myself and my children. I also spent a lot of time fearing my ex-husband would commit suicide like my father had. Whenever he came to get the children, I would hardly say a word, scared that I would upset him. So whenever there was any accommodating to do, any angry or painful feelings toward him, I would keep them to myself.

In therapy I became conscious that I had taken on this super-responsible attitude toward people, and I learned that this was common among children from substance-abusing families. I wasn't alone and I didn't have to hold on to it. It was an old

survival habit from the past. I had the illusion
of having some control over chaos. But I found
it didn't work, anyway, and I gradually learned
to let it go. Divorce brought me to the point
where I finally got rid of this problem.

Ken: One of the many lessons I learned was
about honesty with my family. I thought this
was just something my ex-wife was short on,
but I realized it would have helped, also,
coming from me with my children. At the time
of the divorce I didn't want them to know why
I was leaving their mother. I just couldn't say
"I'm leaving you with a woman who plays
around because I'm somehow no longer her
type." I mean, that's all I could think of then.
So naturally they saw me as the bad guy and
she helped reinforce that. She was the
wounded lady who was left behind.

The kids still have no knowledge of their
mother's affairs, and how I may have failed
her. I didn't just leave because we had some
vague problems. The kids didn't see us argue
much. We weren't close enough to argue.
If I had used counseling and support from the
start, I think I could have been more honest
with them about what really happened. Now
isn't the right time. Some day . . .

Kathy: It's kind of hard now for me to
believe that I thought my life had ended when
Jim headed out. I was only 24! It just shows
how you can get into a habit of thinking of
yourself in only one way. All my teen years,
my friends and I thought about how we looked
almost every waking hour. It never occurred

to us that this wasn't a good attitude to have about ourselves. We thought it showed that we cared about ourselves and about attracting nice guys, not nerds. And it felt so good to be admired. It felt good to be physically active and athletic.

It's obvious to me now that I was really lopsided in what I did and the way I saw myself. Looking good was an easy way to get approval, interest, dates. Whatever else we were or did, I'm sure meant something. I wanted to be known as a nice friendly person. But I gave very little thought to pursuing whatever else I wanted in life. What could be more important than getting a guy? Now I know.

Bob: The drinking thing would have become worse if the divorce hadn't happened. I can't say the divorce wouldn't have happened if I had stopped drinking because that was a symptom of the differences between us, not the cause.

Anyway, I wish I had stopped drinking earlier, both for reasons of health and our relationship. Drinking gave me some temporary relief but it had a permanent effect on my kids' image of me. That's less in their minds, I'm sure, now that alcohol is no longer a part of my life.

THE LOSSES OF DIVORCE

Abraham Lincoln may have never gone through divorce, but he once said about losing companions, "I shall at least have one friend left, and that friend shall be down inside me."

In my own life, the losses have at times appeared
numerous and overwhelming. The prospect of being alone
and a single parent was very frightening. Today in hindsight, I can see that my own experiences with divorce
helped shape that new friend I found "down inside me."

Some of the losses we may encounter after divorce are:

Security	Self-Esteem
Companionship	Comfortable routine
Friends	Finances
Family	Hopes and dreams

At the time, these losses seem to stretch to the horizon
and preoccupy our days. The most distressing immediate
losses I felt were that of family, friends and security. In
1970, divorce was not as common as it is today. Both
friends and family members lacked experience in reacting
to someone who was divorced and they didn't seem to
know how to respond. It was as if a death had taken place:
Many just pulled away. The loneliness and aloneness I
experienced at this time pushed me through the door to
make new friends. What I learned in the process erased a
burden of self-doubt and proved to me that I was capable
of making friends and entering new relationships. There
were many who began to accept me just the way I was.

My loss of financial security began to shape my life
quite drastically. I knew I needed to take responsibility for
myself. I went back to school and started training for a
professional future. Little did I know what was in store
for me as I ventured out, met new people and began my
profession. Today I'm grateful for the push my insecuri-
ties gave me, but back then I didn't have a clue as to the
ultimate fulfillment that would result from the losses I
was experiencing.

When my familiar routine was no more, I was at first
very uncomfortable. Then I began to see that even though
my habits were changed a great deal, there were a host of

advantages presenting themselves. For instance, I no
longer needed to . . .

- Meet the same schedule.
- Fulfill someone elses expectations.
- Hide my emotional pain.
- Be careful in conversation.
- Make excuses.

There was a sense of freedom and opportunity that
was new and empowering. I learned to affirm it frequently, which helped me in the healing process.

As I moved from marital status to single status, there
was quite a shift in self-esteem. At first it seemed like a
loss, but as I met each challenge over and over, my appreciation for what I could do grew and grew. The more I did
well as a single person, the more confident I became in my
own abilities — and the more my self-esteem grew.

REFRAMING OUR LOSSES

Writing down our worries often helps us make them
more manageable. Try sitting down and documenting
what you see as your major losses in the past. Then,
being very honest with yourself, see if you gained anything from them. Usually it can't be said that nothing
positive came out of a loss or that nothing was learned
that didn't benefit our lives later.

ATTITUDE CHOICES:
GOING UP VERSUS GOING DOWN

We all have the option of going one of two ways with
our attitudes after divorce:

Self-Defeating	Self-Esteeming
Blame others: Act as a victim and blame your life problems on someone else.	**Take responsibility:** Let your own values guide you rather than the expectations of others.

Negative attitude:
Emphasize all the down
sides to make things seem
worse than they are.

Lack of focus: Ignore
goals and just live out
others' plans for you.

**Spend time with negative
people:** Pessimism and
criticism are contagious
and will weaken your
potential and self-esteem.

Expect failure: You create
what you believe, so if you
expect to fail, you will.

Take credit: Give yourself
a pat on the back for
your successes and
courage.

Set priorities: Evaluate
your life by what you have,
not by what you don't have.

Make new friends: Look
for people you respect and
become like them. Follow
a positive attitude with
positive behavior.

Expect success: You create
what you believe, so if you
expect to succeed, you will.

Don't talk yourself into feeling as if you have no choices
about your response to divorce. By changing yourself, you
can change your circumstances. That is what empower-
ment is all about. You can choose to turn your losses into
lessons.

Low self-worth people send out
messages of pain. They hide their
feelings under an appearance of
being happy and pleasant.

High self-worth people own all
of their feelings and feel it is
all right to have all feelings. Their
honesty with themselves and others
gives them good feelings.

A high self-worth person is:
  Sometimes happy
  Sometimes angry
  Sometimes sad.
And, whatever the feeling is . . .

We are honest with ourselves.

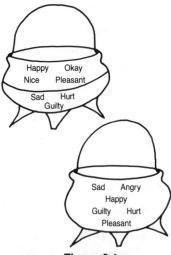

Figure 6.1.
**Pots: Low Self-Worth People
And High Self-Worth People**

STRETCHING YOUR SELF-WORTH

Self-worth, self-esteem, our identity and self-impor-
tance, all are terms describing ways of picturing ourselves.
They are mental photographs of how we think we are
doing on the value scale we have adopted. These images
readily show how much we believe in ourselves.

Virginia Satir developed this concept to make an abstract
idea more concrete by looking at self-worth in terms of a
pot — a three-legged, round, huge, black iron pot. During
winter the pot is used to store potatoes. During summer,
vegetables and meat are put in the pot for making stew.
Another time in the year, it is used for making soap. Two
questions always came to mind about the pot and its con-
tents: What is it full of now and how full is it?

This pot image is open to many interpretations. One
implication from the image of pot as self-worth is that a
healthy relationship is based on reality. We need to face
who we are and how much the other person can realistically give.

Another idea apparent from the illustration is that
high-pot people can choose to be generous and positive:
They have a lot to give. Low-pot people tend to protect,
to guard what little of themselves they have, especially
by keeping others far enough away so that no one can see
their inadequacies. Their isolation makes them fearful
but it is necessary to keep alive the impression that they
are generous.

Another interpretation is that the different ingredients
in the pot have varied effects on others. Soap and stew
give off good smells and attract people in friendly gatherings. Friendliness is expressed in the sharing of oneself
with others after they have shared the products from the
pot. People add vegetables and meat. People share the
stew in friendship.

Potatoes, on the other hand, when they have been
stored too long, can rot and have a rather offensive odor.

People want them out of their lives. The pot of neglected potatoes is similar to behavior which keeps people away. The level of one's self-worth gives out messages. It is similar to the quantity and quality of materials in our pot.

CHOICES TO CHANGE, BROADEN SECURITY

Grabbing the opportunity to make choices is an exciting part of our divorce recovery. We will make some mistakes, but if we keep trying and risking, many new possibilities will come into our life.

We cannot expect ourselves to move forward all at once. We will, in time, develop the confidence that we will recover wholeness.

Security will broaden. Security is a basic need for each of us. Even with a divorce, our security cannot be taken away because it is based on our belief in ourselves and only *we* own that belief. Security is grounded not only in our capacity to cope and survive but in our ability to make choices.

As we trust ourselves, we find our security becoming more firm.

7

Most Ex-Spouses Agree: Divorce Is A Positive Force

Joan: Sometimes I think it's good we can't see ahead. We'd be overwhelmed. Still, I wish I had known at the time of my divorce how many doors it was going to open for me. I never would have believed it. I went back to school, got two degrees and became a professional. I never planned on that happening. I never thought I had the ability to do that. As a result of that and all the other things that happened to me, I feel it made me a much more whole person. I reach out to people much more now. I don't feel nervous if I'm not in control of everything.

After I started believing in myself, I came to a much greater realization of the ultimate goodness of the whole universe. When I opened myself to opportunities, they came. It

made me believe in a master plan for all of us.
I started allowing myself the luxury of finding
out what my plan was all about. In a way, my
divorce led to a new sense of spirituality.

Ken: My divorce really opened my eyes.
It was a case of better late than never. I had
been really stuck in a role with a lifestyle
everyone approved of, but some part of reality
was missing. I had always thought that an
important part of being successful was having
a beautiful woman at my side. Okay, so the
woman is gone but, not only that, everything I
worked for went with her. Of course, that was
my own decision, but there I was with nothing
that I thought mattered anymore. So I either
had to convince myself that *I* still mattered or
just wallow in my losses. It was a clear-cut
choice and the wallowing was hurting my
work.

I had to get over the idea that I was coming
home to an empty apartment. It wasn't empty.
I was there! Counseling helped me reinforce
that. Being by myself really became okay.
Being myself — looking and feeling my best,
doing what I want to — well, to me that is
gratifying now.

Kathy: Divorce was a stretch. It forced me
into taking action. I never felt I had special
abilities for a career. But I went back to school
because I knew I had to make a living and
college graduates get better pay. I took a
computer course because everything's about
computers now, and I was surprised. I liked
computers. I went into computer

programming, and I also found I had other skills. Management, for one. I really turned on to the whole process of getting ahead, getting a good job. And I did.

For the first time in my life, I felt as if I could be independent. I wasn't waiting to go out with some popular guy now as my big thing. I was doing less dating than in high school. And now I'm getting less exercise, although that's still real important for me. But I'm far more conscious now of the fact that I'm more than how I look.

Bob: I still have a letter from my attorney stating that he had to put in writing his opposition to my decision to give up everything and that it ran against his advice. He said he felt it was a very poor move. That's an understatement. If I had it to do over again — heaven forbid — I would go to counseling first to get a stronger sense of self-worth. I needed approval too much from everyone. And I didn't think my needs were at all important. Then there was the guilt thing. If I hadn't made her pull up roots, maybe my wife wouldn't have started running around. But maybe she would have anyway.

The AA community did a great deal for me. I met people there who valued me. If I had concentrated earlier on other friends who weren't such drinkers, I would have avoided some problems. The negativity of my old friends in the past had dragged me down. But I had been too busy and lazy back then to make new friends.

The reality has set in. A future full of question marks looms ahead. Now's the time when we'd really like to hear from others who have walked this way before us. What do both the leavers and the left have to say about this crisis of divorce after they've reached the ranks of survivors?

In my work as a therapist I have surveyed 200 people about their divorces and what influences divorce had in their lives. Over the years I have worked with many couples who have been through various stages of relationship. Some have divorced; some have remarried; some are adult children from divorced families. Among their responses I have looked for patterns that might help others in healing from painful relationships and the divorce process. There is a general agreement about the best advice to give the recently separated, and about the benefits that divorce ultimately produce. While they admitted it wasn't all easy and upbeat, the majority of those who responded felt divorce was a positive occurrence in their lives.

As we all agree, there's no doubt divorce is one of the most painful and emotionally draining events in a lifetime. But as the shock, the hurt and the numbness begin to subside, the ability to function does return. Function then leads to adjustment. This adjustment is the direct result of taking action. This action springs from allowing movement and transition to happen, rather than clinging to dreams and worn-out patterns.

EX-SPOUSES' REACTIONS AND ADVICE

Divorce recovery takes time. We grow a little each day, despite not being able to make the great leaps and bounds we'd like to. Here are eight of the ways ex-spouses in the survey reacted to the main issues of divorce:

1. Get clear about your own contribution to the marriage and the divorce. Recognize that when a divorce takes place, both parties have contributed to the deterioration of the relationship. As we look at our own part of the problem, blame gets reduced. When there is less blame, it becomes easier to negotiate, adjust and move on.

A second reason to explore one's own role is that everything learned about our own part in the coming together, the life shared and the reasons for the divorce will come in handy if we enter into another relationship.

2. Avoid entering another relationship for a year. There are so many emotional merry-go-rounds you will ride as a part of the divorce that it's good to give intense feelings a rest before going into another relationship. Right after having surgery, would you go on a hiking vacation? Let your emotional healing happen before taking on intense and important feelings in a new close friendship.

3. Develop a support system. A divorce often changes social networks. Some couples' friends feel as though they have to take sides. Some relatives of one's ex-partner may change their attitudes. It's important to start your own support system free of entanglements.

During this time, if at all possible, join a support group in your area. There are many different kinds of groups.

The best move you can make is to contact a therapist. A therapist can help you find either a therapy group or a support group, in addition to serving as your sounding board. You can take all your hurt, anger and any other feelings you might be experiencing to therapy. A therapist's training can help you put it all together to obtain a new perspective.

Making new friends should be on your agenda, too. Reach out and share life with new people.

4. Face Reality. Not facing reality is why most marriages end. There comes a time to look at matters the way they are and not the way we wish they were. So often we hang on to a remote hope, a thread or a myth. At some point it becomes necessary to sever that last fragile link and transfer energy from hanging on to letting go.

5. Be willing to face difficult times with children. Children are in a tough spot in all divorces. There are various issues of concern, such as money, loyalty or feelings. Keeping your issues, feelings and needs quite separate from those of your children will help. It is critical to let them know their needs are important, but don't lose sight of the fact that this is *your* divorce. If you meet your own needs, you will be a stronger, more able person to meet theirs. If you don't, no one will be happy.

Children need to know that it is going to take time to work out everyone's needs. Meanwhile you can be the role model they'll need later in life by equipping yourself in all ways to function best as head of the family.

6. Take the opportunity to grow in self-worth. Self-worth comes, in part, from knowing you can care for yourself. Regardless of your past sense of self-worth, divorce offers the opportunity to develop a healthy opinion of who you are. During divorce recovery we are catapulted into an opportunity that demands we develop every resource we have. As we succeed, we feel better and better about ourselves. These good feelings will foster and increase self-worth.

Here are some comments on self-worth from people in my survey:

Eilene, 36: "Re-establishing myself has begun a new adventure in life."

John, 54: "I faced myself, hit bottom and started up. I panicked, I fell and picked myself up. Today I fly strong and bold, surrounded by people who like me. And I like myself."

Jill, 48: "I feel good about myself and my achievements."

Bonnie, 39: "My self-esteem has greatly improved since achieving success independently."

Cynthia, 48: "I learned to become a whole person. I learned to take risks. Today I like who I am and learn to love myself more each day."

Nicole, 47: "I am able to see my growth both personally and professionally. I have many new supportive friends."

Mitchell, 43: "My self-worth is fantastic now."

Toby, 36: "Today I have found myself. Prior to the divorce I was only someone's daughter, wife, mother."

Ray, 37: "Because of the activities I was forced to undertake, and did so successfully, I have become a much stronger, confident person."

7. Develop fulfilling relationships. The majority of people responding to the survey highlighted the importance of developing honest, direct and nurturing relationships. It's important to invest time and energy in as many family relationships as possible. There are siblings, aunts, uncles and grandparents who also become involved in the family changes. Whenever you can, keep and nurture relationships. The more support you have, the faster you will heal. On the other hand, if the relationships are blaming and add more pain and stress to your life, you may need to let them go.

When developing new relationships you may want to look for mentors as well as support: people you'd like to have share their secrets of success with you. These may be people you can talk to or people you see or hear about whose achievements in the face of obstacles can be recalled for inspiration.

Here are some comments from the people in my survey on the value of relationships in divorce recovery:

Ted, 43: "I have found friends who accept me."

Fay, 29: "I have more honest relationships with my children."

Yvonne, 51: "I have learned to know the value of three or four good friends rather than lots of acquaintances."

Andrea, 36: "I have made new friends who support me in my struggles, have fun with me and help me celebrate my victories."

8. Face and express your feelings. There are many feelings to be felt and expressed during this very tumultuous time. Feelings that do not get expressed become painful attitudes that are self-defeating.

- Anger not expressed becomes *depression.*
- Hurt not expressed becomes permanent *sadness.*
- Fears not expressed become *avoidance.*
- Inadequacies not expressed become *phoney smiles.*

All feelings have purpose. Feel them, and in a safe nurturing place, express them. This is where the value of support groups and a therapist becomes important. Expressing deep and painful feelings must be done, and yet it's not appropriate to share many of these feelings with children, relatives and friends. Even closest friends do not want to know the depth of some feelings.

Through my survey of ex-spouses I heard about much healing as time passed:

Libby, 49: "I was so angry in the early days. I'm grateful I was able to express that anger to my therapist and turn my energy toward my own growth."

Angela, 40: "I thought I was going to cry forever. Then one day, I dried my tears and went on. Some days a special song or holiday will bring tears again, but most of the time I feel great."

Cristy, 38: "My fears of loneliness have really been relieved in the last few months. In the beginning, I think I felt lonely because of all the change. I don't feel that way anymore."

Tom, 50: "My early hurt healed as I looked more closely at what happened. I could more easily see both of our contributions. My hurt turned to sadness and today that sadness has healed."

MY OWN (AND OTHERS') BEST RECOVERY TOOLS

1. Good friends. Making the time to see friends was crucial for me. I lost some and gained some, but the friends who stuck with me were the most honest and sincere.

2. Prayer. There were some times when only faith in God could comfort me and it was what I sought. While I hated much of the divorce process, I found peace and comfort in developing a spiritual life for myself. Now that some distance has been achieved, I can see that there was much sense and order in all that happened. I am grateful for my growth and the belief I have in spirituality. Whatever name you give to a Higher Power, drawing on this spiritual source can be an antidote for the initial loneliness and powerlessness we experience.

3. Asking for help. I used to think I could do everything by myself. Today I know that this personal myth is part of my belief that no one was trustworthy, that no one would be there for me. During the divorce crisis I learned to ask, receive and accept help. Most of the people I have talked to expressed just how wonderful being able to reach out was for them.

4. Relief from indecision and tension. Many of the ex-spouses in my survey reported that there had been months (sometimes years) of anxiety and stress coming from indecision. I, too, was afraid of making mistakes and vacillated over what action to take until I was a wreck. Finally I learned that very few mistakes are irreversible and that when I did act, action brought relief and more energy. In time I also learned to trust myself — only because I acted and saw the results, which were usually just fine. It took action to prove I could trust in myself.

5. Books, tapes, workshops. The bookstores are full of guides and help for people who want to grow and change. Many people in my survey reported they got a great deal of support and direction from the printed word. Weekend and week-long workshops were mentioned by over half of my respondents as a help in skill building.

6. Developing new hobbies and recreations. Again, almost everyone I heard from has started new activities for themselves. These activities helped to relieve stress, divert attention from problems and offer opportunities to meet new friends. Not to mention providing pleasure. Activities people mentioned as positive included:

- Dancing
- Music lessons
- Fly fishing
- Traveling
- Volunteer work
- Horseback riding

7. Exploring your family-of-origin issues. This certainly is high on my list of ways to make progress personally. More than half of the people I surveyed said that divorce raised questions about the past that prompted exploration. As this questioning took place, my surveyed ex-spouses reported that they were learning about themselves in a way that had not been available to them earlier.

Divorce brings many old family patterns to the surface. When we look at, and learn to understand, childhood emotional baggage that we are still carrying, we see the origins of many misunderstandings. It has been said by many marriage and family therapists that innumerable divorces could have been prevented if the partners had previously divorced their family of origin. This is not to say that families were to blame; it only indicates that there is much to be learned from detaching from family patterns.

8. Taking care of your body. Sometimes after divorce we are very vulnerable to practices that are bad for our bodies, and I was no exception. When feelings are troubled, it is easy to overeat or undereat. Sometimes depression stalls our exercise efforts. Respondents to my survey reported that they felt most healthy and strong when they ate well, slept enough and exercised regularly.

Some got new haircuts. Many reported that getting rid of old clothes and choosing a new look helped a great deal. Since many people miss the actual physical touch and presence of the person who was in their lives, three-quarters of the surveyed ex-spouses said a massage enjoyed periodically helped fill that void. Today most health clubs offer professional massage to their members, making it a convenient way of pampering ourselves.

WAYS WE HAVE GROWN

Divorcing ex-partners commented in the survey on how much better they thought their lives had become after divorcing. Fay said, "Since my divorce, and all the emotions it's brought out among us, I have been able to be more open with each of my children. We talk about real and practical things. They come to me more easily and share themselves with me. The tension in our home is relieved and communication has become more open."

With Marianne, financial independence became a pleasure: "To be totally responsible for myself, to be able to do it, gives me a great deal of self-worth. It feels so free to be in charge of my time, my work and my money. I feel like an independent, whole person."

Wynne appreciated learning how to take care of both physical and emotional needs without a live-in partner: "No longer do I depend on someone to make me happy. I've learned how to get my needs met, how to make friends and how to care for myself. I've grown to respect and appreciate myself."

WHAT PARENTS LEARNED TO TELL THEIR CHILDREN ABOUT DIVORCE

Children are often a mysterious and troubling complication to the newly divorced. What to tell them? What to *do* about them? I asked survey participants to share advice they wished their children had received at the time of the divorce. They would have counseled them sooner to . . .

"Stay out of the middle!"

"The divorce is between your parents. You will never know all that went on with your parents," one father said he would have told his boys. One mom did tell her daughter, "Each of us will need a separate relationship with you. Do your best to give us that chance to have different ways, different rules."

"Do not carry messages!"

"Be clear with each parent that you want to be yourself with them, not the voice of someone else, and if that is going to be possible, then you cannot carry messages between them." Message carrying leads to various forms of trouble, many ex-spouses agreed.

"Find a good safe friend to share with!"

Parents wished their children had more people to turn to than just them, such as a peer, a teacher, a relative or an adult friend recommended by the parent. "Find someone you can trust and share your feelings with that person," one ex-spouse advised her 14-year-old daughter. "You need someone besides your parents to share with. This is important for you."

"Accept that you have been through a big trauma. Find as much help as you need to adjust to it and become stronger."

Parents in the survey thought that children if at all possible, should have professional care, such as a therapist, a support group or a school counselor. Jean, a mother of three, told her children, "It's okay to get some ideas from a counselor when your life is changing, when it's feeling strange and you are confused."

"Tell yourself each day: The divorce is between your parents and is not your fault."

If your children remember only one thing about their parents' parting, this should be it. Because child-rearing problems are so often mentioned in predivorce arguments, children need to know that their parents' problems were not about them but about one another.

Children who are encouraged to take advantage of various sources of help are likely to reach out sooner as adults and not carry crippling emotional burdens in order to prove their self-worth. They will learn that no matter how much input they get from others, they themselves must remain in charge of learning and acting on the advice that feels right for them.

8

Helping Children Cope With Divorce

Joan: I think the effects of divorce on children can be both positive and negative. If you gave away your right to child support as I did, you have to work hard to give them things, and work even harder to make time for them. My remarriage solved the companionship problem but since my second husband wasn't earning a lot, I still needed to put in many hours at work.

I took my three kids into my second marriage. I was very fortunate that my second husband really loved them, even though he wasn't in a position to help support them. But he was there for them emotionally and physically. My job took me away from home a lot so this was good in one sense. In another sense I lost out on some of the important years

with my children. But they did have a good
male influence, and even after my second
marriage ended in divorce, he remained good
friends with my children for some of the
critical years.

Ken: After divorcing, I messed up with the
kids during their teens. I had a daughter and
three boys. I really overprotected them,
bought them everything. I got my daughter
involved in my business. She wanted to make
some money, and we got along well. She met
all my business associates and was an asset to
me. She became very protective of me,
controlling my hours, my eating and making
sure I took care of myself. That felt good, to
be taken care of again, but as time passed, it
became too much. It even got in the way of my
relationship with my boys. If they needed
something from me, she'd tell them I was busy
and not let me know. Things like that began
to happen.

So I went back to counseling. It was almost
like going through another divorce, but I had
to get some breathing space for my life. My
daughter wound up in counseling, too. Awful
as it all was, I'd say we both learned a lot about
ourselves that will come in handy in the
future.

Kathy: Four years after my divorce I
married Karl. He had two young children, ages
five and seven. I hadn't really been on my own
very long when I found myself with three new
people in my life. In the summer we were all
together. During the school year we shared

custody with the children's mother. This
caused all kinds of difficulties but we had
plenty of good times, too.

   I knew there would be many things to learn
about being a Mom with children past the
toddler stages. The main thing I figured out
is that the first people to consider are my
husband and myself when troubles come up. If
we can keep our relationship clear, and are
open and honest with one another, it seems
like together we can handle almost any
problems with the kids. When we aren't this
way, then almost any problem can divide us.
Becoming more of my own person gave me a
better idea of how families should work. I
know my priorities now.

   Bob: I had lots of problems with the kids,
but most of them resulted from the bitterness
of the divorce. My ex was very vocal and
aggressive in letting the children know how
she felt about their father. This, of course, put
the kids in a very awkward position. I had to
defend myself, which meant putting her down.
Otherwise I felt I'd be seen as a total wimp.
   My daughter says she has the hardest time
in her own arguments with people because she
doesn't know what to say or do except walk
away. She's in counseling and that's helping. I
think my kids are going to work out what they
need to do. I've come to terms with not being
able to role-model every single issue positively
for them. I'm human and they'll be human as
parents, too. But I'm glad that I've set an
example for my boys about getting help when
things get out of hand.

RECOVERY FOR CHILDREN
OF DIVORCE

When children are made aware that divorce is becoming a reality, their number one need is to feel secure and blameless. Their world — seemingly beyond their control — is toppling and, more than you suspect, they are probably aware of the history of arguments and growing loss of affection.

ADDRESS THEIR NEEDS

They desperately need you to help reduce the trauma with reassurances that . . .

- It is not their fault.
- The divorce is between both parents, not parents and children.
- They will be safe in terms of home, money and school; no more surprises.
- You will love them no matter what.
- You want to hear their feelings.
- You will tell them what's going on that concerns them.
- You can't fix everything.

These are the basics of safety during divorce recovery for children. Whether children are young, adolescent or adult, they are part of a divorce process. Their emotional involvements need to be addressed and shouldn't be minimized, despite the difficulties involved. Very often the children aren't informed that the parents' divorce is in the offing. Including them early in the separation lets them get used to the idea gradually, reducing shock. They need ample assurance that your love for them is secure and can't go away. Children are especially emotional about divorce, but studies show they are also resilient after it occurs.

For many people, a divorce means that their relationship with their partner has been totally and completely ended. That is how it needs to be in many cases for practical and emotional reasons. However, there are many people for whom divorce means some continued contact, particularly if the couple share children of any age. We, as divorced parents, can benefit tremendously by getting a head start on what can be expected in parenting after divorce, both in our roles as single parents and when our ex-spouse becomes involved.

COMMUNICATE RIGHT FROM THE START

When the first steps toward divorce are taken, we need to be able to tell our children that things are not going well between us and our spouses, tough as it may be. This will give the children a chance to grieve appropriately for their changing family. Although it is not a pleasant prospect, it is one that we should not try to prevent. Prolonging the news until the last minute and then suddenly confronting a child with the physical realities of the split is more of a shock. Explain to the child what is happening and in words that children can understand; all the details don't have to be spelled out. Be honest about your feelings. Tell them that you're sad, that you're hurt. Tell them that you, as parents, are not agreeing about many things and you no longer love each other in the same way you did before.

About 65 to 70 percent of all the children I have worked with felt that, one way or another, they were part of their parents' divorce. Children need to know that they didn't cause this problem and they cannot fix it either. Make it very, very clear to them that the divorce is between the adults and not between parents and children. This understanding is crucial to the child's self-worth.

AFFIRM YOUR LOVE FOR THEM

Find ways to affirm your children on a daily basis. Maybe you need to say to them, "I love you just the way you are." And, "I cherish the fact that you are with me as we all go through this together."

Support one another. Saying, "You are the most important thing in my life right now" will win a response you
need. Continue to let them know they are cherished and
loved, and that your feelings for them are *not* going to
change.

Children may worry that you could stop loving *them*,
too. They should hear that there was a time when the
parents loved each other a whole lot and that they were
born out of that love . . . but things change for adults.
Even though Mom and Dad do not love each other in the
way that they need to as a husband and a wife, *nothing* can
change the love of their own children.

EXPECT DENIAL AND ALLOW HEALING

Parents can expect that their children may deny the fact
of divorce for a while. Denial is a natural protective process that often occurs whenever a death takes place.
Divorce, in many ways, is like a death in the family. Let
them deny the situation, but keep letting them know your
feelings and a little bit of what's going on.

Eventually you may be able to hire a family counselor
or a children's counselor to come in and spend special time
with the children. There are all kinds of possibilities to
address the issues of feelings and divorce with children.

Children *can* take the news and get on with the business
of being a child. They will not only recover and be fine
when they are eight years old, but they'll be fine when
they are 28. Divorce happens to one million kids each
year. Within four years, 80 percent of their parents under
45 remarry. These changes bring new people into a child's
life. Stepparenting and blended families are frequent. It is
not just ties to parents that are left and remade; ties to
grandparents, friends, aunts, uncles and other relatives
change. Through all of this children can sail confidently
if their self-esteem is powered with love, expressed
frequently.

>
> *Living so much in the present as they do, kids don't know that time makes things better. Reassure them that change happens and that happiness — like summer vacations and holidays — returns in time.*

PARENTAL COOPERATION

Some of the inevitable changes and events in the lives of children will help heal the problems around divorce. Both parents very likely will want to be present, harmoniously, for children at graduations, school programs, weddings, births, baptisms and bas and bar mitzvahs. Each of these times provides an opportunity for parents to show their children that they want to support and honor them. Their presence says that what went on between the parents is private, between them, but each parent will continue to be there for the child. This kind of cooperation in itself is healing for children. If the parents are willing to make some of these concessions, independence and maturity can be strengthened for the children by watching their divorced parents.

> *Parenting tends to be for life, even though marriages aren't always.*

In addition to hearing that both parents will never stop loving them, children need to know that there will be continuous interaction for years, and that both parents are committed to their emotional and financial well-being.

There will be many different times and ways that divorced parents will be required to talk to one another and negotiate again. If they can keep open the lines of communication, share parental decisions and retain an appropriate level of respect, they will minimize the effects of divorce on the children. Sometimes we are so estranged from our ex-spouses that we need a third party available at all discussions about our children. Sometimes we can learn to negotiate together reasonably, but a counselor may be able to help us do it more easily. Whatever difficulties we might have, they will work out best if they are brought out on the table and if negotiated solutions are regarded as binding by both parties.

Often, because of my work, I spend a great deal of time traveling and in airports. There I frequently see a painful picture of the younger children of divorce trudging along, hand in a parent's, carrying their duffle bags of commuting toys and clothes to one of their two homes. These children know that in one house the plates are on high shelves and in the other house the plates are on low shelves. In one place they have a bed of their own, and in another they may share a bed with a sibling. For these transient youngsters, life is like learning to live with constant culture shock as they travel between two "foreign countries," with different "languages," different rules, different expectations and different lifestyles. Sometimes these children go through unnecessary suffering because the parents, in their own pain, often don't see the needs of their children.

For commuting children of divorced parents, travel is no vacation. Adjusting to the different "cultures" of their two homes can be stressful. Parents need to acknowledge the children's situation, encouraging and praising their flexibility, which will aid them later in adulthood.

Parental cooperation can ease the trials of children who must change homes periodically. Parents need to be aware of the difficulty in shifting over to a different order and remember their child's age and stage of development.

SEPARATING FACT FROM FANTASY

When past relationships within the family have been painful, we may come away with bitterness. However, when we dwell on how our families were happy or were perceived to be happy, we can develop unreal fantasies as we idealize the past. We might choose to remember that our life was always about vacations, such as Disney World, and good food on the table. In fact, the parents may have tilted appearances one way or the other, but the truth was quite different.

> *Parents can help children remember that there were both good things and painful things about the past — and there will be some good things and some hurtful things about the future.*

DON'T PUT MESSAGES IN MONEY

Often money becomes tighter as people need to change their lifestyles. Sometimes money gets easier. What is significant is that money should not be used with children to demonstrate approval or punishment. The parent with the most money tries to buy the children's devotion, loyalty and love. Disconnect these emotions from dollar signs in your children's eyes at every opportunity.

LOYALTY

In crisis and stress children may feel a lot of shame about what is happening with their parents. Often they feel a strong sense of loyalty toward one or both. When they are being pulled both ways, sometimes they find the only person they can talk to is a therapist. In therapy children often realize for the first time that what they are feeling is anger and hurt. If their loyalty to their parents is acted out at the children's expense, they may need to learn to love themselves enough to say no to painful conflicts.

SHARING AND STRETCHING SPECIAL DATES

As visits, holidays and times with each parent are worked out, children should be kept out of listening range. They can be made to feel like bartered objects. There are many optional ways of dealing with this. Some people have Christmas on a different date. Some celebrate birthdays one year with one family, one year with the next. Each of the children can have some vacation time with each parent. Insisting on the observance of a special event on a conflicting date isn't nearly as important to a child as not being the subject of discord between their parents.

CHILDHOOD CHALLENGES OF DIVORCE
CAN BENEFIT ADULTHOOD

There are some behavioral experts who think the adversity of divorce, with its challenges, actually has a positive effect on children, and that some of them end up being wiser and learning more about love because they have suffered loss. Perhaps they may even turn out more creative. According to *Business Week* (September 30, 1985):

Creative people usually don't have dull, predictable childhoods. Instead, childhood is marked by exposure to diversity. Strains in family life, financial ups and downs or divorces are common. Experts believe a dose of diversity gives children the ability to see issues and problems from different points of view. Creative types are generally independent and highly motivated. They are also great skeptics, risk takers and thinkers. Disorder does not make them anxious. Indeed, they relish it.

Be gentle with yourself and your children. They, too, are experiencing trauma and need understanding support. Divorce presents a special opportunity for increased bonding with children.

YOUNGSTERS AREN'T ALWAYS DISTURBED BY DIVORCE

Leading up to many divorces are times of "cold war," "the silent treatment," loud, dish-throwing fights, sometimes even physical violence, and sometimes pure silent abandonment. Children feel what is going on, whether it is directed at them or not, and whether or not they are brought into the prime action.

Often divorce is a relief that can lessen anxieties and remove uncomfortable or scary feelings. Children will become much less nervous in an atmosphere of peace and less likely to seek too much diversion outside of the home.

KIDS WITH TWO HOMES OFTEN BENEFIT

The ideal situation is to live full-time in one home, but consider other possibilities as equally beneficial:

1. If children have contact with two parents, they have a sense of security in two places, rather than just one. They also have a broader perspective about life and realize there is not just one way of looking at things. They are exposed to more than one set of values and have an opportunity to combine and create their own.

2. The two homes may offer an expanded network of support. At each home there may be a different set of relatives who now show up, new neighbors and children to play with. Two home sites may have many more options than one.

Whether a family remains intact in a first marriage, whether it becomes modified into a single-parent family

or whether a remarried blended family becomes the home,
the following remains a classic truth:

> *In unhealthy families, children are there to meet
> the needs of their parents, to entertain, serve or
> glorify. In healthy families, parents are there to
> meet the essential needs of their children,
> physically and emotionally.*

SOME SIGNS OF SUCCESS IN DIVORCED HOMES WITH HAPPY KIDS

1. *Children are encouraged to form their own non-biased
   opinions* of all parents and step-parents. Parents neither sugarcoat nor blame the other parent.
2. *Parents encourage expression* of anger, hurt, loneliness,
   fears and tears from the children.
3. *Scheduling conflicts are handled by parents,* and children
   are not put in the middle of the stress and strain.
4. *Children have role models of happy relationships.* Each
   parent either provides this with a new partner or
   spends time with the kids and other families where
   these relationships exist.
5. *Each parent affirms each child's self-worth* as often as
   possible to reinforce the reality that divorce ends a
   marriage, not the parent-child bond. Children of all
   ages need to hear:
   • I'm glad you are my son/daughter.
   • You are special.
   • I like spending time with you.
   • I love you.
6. *Parents keep good boundaries* about their own divorce
   concerns. Many family therapists believe that 80
   percent of parents' personal business is none of the
   children's business. Too often children will take on

responsibility for what they know. Most of a parent's stress and conflict does not need to be known by the child.

7. *Parents don't try to do everything for their children.* Children do not need super-parents. This only causes inadequacy and role modeling that creates anxiety.

8. *Parents keep a sense of humor.* Children need help in knowing there are at least two sides to everything. They need help to develop their sense of humor and to "lighten up." Seeing that their parents can be happy, whether single or postdivorce, is an inspiration.

Parents are to parent *children; children are to* be *children.*

AS CHILDREN MATURE

There will be many situations that will require special negotiation and consideration as children grow up. In a healthy family, parents and children take the time and attention to work these out to the best advantage for each person involved. In a healthy family, compromise and negotiations become an important part of day-to-day living. In a painful family, situations become opportunities for control and power struggles. There is more emphasis on winning and being right than there is on finding solutions.

Painful And Healthy Family Relationships

Painful	Healthy
Major focus on one member.	All are heard and considered.
Children are expected to meet the needs of the parent.	Parents are expected to meet the needs of the children.
Lots of secrets.	Openness and honesty.

Parents *tell* children how to live.	Parents *show* children how to live.
Everyone in the family is involved in the business of the other.	Each family member is given space and privacy with respectful boundaries.
There is loyalty to each family member, even if not deserved.	Members are able to choose how or whether to stay actively related.
Shame-based people, low self-worth in each family member.	Mistakes, making up and forgiveness are taught and accepted.
Gloom and frequent depression or sadness prevent a happy family atmosphere.	The family has a good time together, with joy, a sense of humor and laughter.

FLEXIBILITY

As families mature, there will need to be many more changes in keeping with the times. Riding with these changes makes life easier for both you and the children. Several areas in which adjustments will be made over the years are:

1. Money management. As mentioned earlier, sometimes there is less money available following a divorce. Some suggestions in regard to finances: One or both parents provide the necessities for the children (housing, medical care, food, daily support). Then for larger purchases (braces, graduation, wedding expenses, car insurance, trips), both parents contribute. Later on the child can become an additional contributor. Realizing the amount of negotiation and interaction that will continue long after the divorce, parents should try to maintain as much ability to communicate with one another as possible from the start.

2. *Feelings will go up and down.* Riding an emotional roller coaster is normal. The more children talk about all the feelings they have, the easier it will be to let go of the feelings that they don't want.

- ANGER . . .
    at the parent who started the divorce.
    at the parent who leaves.
    at the parent who stays.
- FEAR . . .
    of needing to move and sometimes change schools.
    of what other kids will say.
    of needing to take care of a parent.
    of parents no longer loving them.
    of not enough money.
    of losing a parent.
- GUILT . . .
    over having contributed to the divorce.
- SADNESS . . .
    over losing access to grandparents.
    over losing two-parent family vacations.

Depression, rage or hysteria in children can be the result of inadequately expressed feelings that build over time. Children should be encouraged that feeling angry is natural and that it's all right to cry. During a divorce, it's normal to have times of hurt, sadness and loss. They need to be told that it's important to express emotions and to express them when they are first felt.

With very young children, sometimes sharing feelings can be done in the context of telling or reading a story and reflecting on the feelings. Even before children are able to read or write, they are able to draw pictures — another way for children to express their feelings. Later, as soon as youngsters are old enough to read, help them pick out books about divorce at the library or bookstore. Look for magazine articles with items about divorce. It makes children feel better to know they aren't the only ones going through this experience.

Checking with your children's school may reassure you that there are resource people and support groups for children of divorce. If the school doesn't have these services, you may want to start one. Perhaps your house could be the place where the children could gather. The get-together can be leaderless, with children simply talking about the difficulties they are facing. Or you might want to plan some group activities to help them release the stresses of divorce.

3. Child custody battles have no winners. Regardless of how we might like it to be, if there are children involved in a divorce, there are blood ties that are going to last forever, way beyond the end of child support at 18. When a child gets married at the age of 25 or 26, that's a family affair. When the first child is born to your child and you and your ex-spouse now have to share grandchildren, that's a family affair. When there is a terminal illness, a crisis or a trauma in the lives of one or the other parent, that is a family affair. The luckiest children will be those who are allowed to have whatever experiences they need to have with either parent, without interference or criticism.

A wonderful book to help parents struggling with custody issues is *Divorced Families: Meeting The Challenge Of Divorce And Remarriage* by Constance B. Ahrons, Ph.D. (Norton, 1987).

4. Changing rituals and relationships. Meals, exercise, friendships, guests in the house, school events — any of these daily encounters may have to be renegotiated with our children. Some rituals, such as holidays and vacations, may have to be scaled down or the dates altered, but only the positives should be emphasized.

PAINFUL TIMES FOR FAMILIES

In my divorce survey, parents uniformly agreed that

Thanksgiving, Christmas and Hanukkah were highly stressful and possibly painful times for families. Holidays tend to bring out the best and worst in relationships.

Be prepared to handle your children's nostalgic emotions that may arise during holidays. Following are some ways to deal with these emotional incidents.

THANKSGIVING

This holiday signals the beginning of a season that can bring sadness as well as joy to divorced families. It's a time for nostalgia, when many of us reflect on the good times we used to have as a family. The rituals we observe on this holiday provide us with a sense of continuity year after year. Families come together and share turkey, dressing, cranberry sauce, sweet potatoes, pumpkin pie — all of our traditional holiday foods.

But all things change, and Thanksgiving is no exception. It was once a time when the food brought to the table was hunted by the men and grown in home gardens by the family. It was a time when families ground their own grain, pressed apples for cider and made their own butter. As that era has passed, so has another. We can commemorate the old times but we can also update Thanksgiving and make it a holiday tradition much more focused on the present and the future.

Adopting and adapting are happening everywhere today with the Thanksgiving meal. A light salad and fresh vegetables may replace some of the traditional items, and rich desserts may be substituted with low-cal ones, such as a pumpkin souffle. We can even take the entire event and make it a time of celebration with new habits. Rather than everyone sitting around watching football after dinner, everyone could go to the fitness club or take a long leisurely walk together, reflecting on what the year has brought.

As we sit around a different-looking holiday table, we could talk about changes with our children: How there is more than one breadwinner in a family now; how we have the convenience of microwaves and ovens for quick and easy baking; and how other convenience foods (well-loved by children) have changed our lifestyle from those of previous times.

Figure 8.1. Holidays

Holidays will continue to be fun if families allow themselves to remake traditions.

And, by the way, a reality check may be in order. Perhaps the past history of holiday time wasn't a rosy as we long to remember it. Were there tensions that nobody wanted to talk about? Unspoken feelings always hanging in the air? As we try to improve our lives through this process of divorce, we may take this holiday and move forward with it, knowing we are celebrating in harmony, with all of us wanting to be there. We can be free with feelings and thoughts, and the self-worth of each person will be honored. Let's go for a lighter meal, a lighter touch and lots of love.

Our harvest is in. We have a lot to be thankful for.

CHRISTMAS AND HANUKKAH

These are the "Big Ones." Throughout our family life together, all of our Christmases are supposed to be "bright," just as the song says. You might not make it home for Thanksgiving, but Christmas and Hanukkah are definitely watersheds of family feelings. Because people's memories come tumbling back one way or another at this time of year, it is a season loaded with bygones, personal histories and sometimes myths. Any holiday has a hard time living up to our expectations. Is it any wonder that during the holiday season the suicide rate and hospital admissions for depression are so high? Realism and idealism collide on the day after, and many people are left saying, "Is that all there is?"

When we have gone through a divorce or our family has become a divorced family, it's to our advantage to plan ahead for these "delicate" days. First of all, you may need to revise the calendar. When children are to be shared during the season, get the whole family into the mood of flexible fun. For example, there is nothing that you do on December 25th that can't be done on some other day. You can easily work out which weekend in December will be holiday-celebration time for which group of relatives.

There is no law saying you can't have Christmas fun on the second, third or fourth weekend in December, as well as the actual date of the 25th. In our family, celebrations have been rearranged so that we can count on Christmas coming the second weekend in December. We have had many wonderful Christmases in this way, with our very own special calendar. This leaves two more weekends, plus Christmas itself, during which we can share the spirit with other members of our extended or divorced families.

There are many benefits that come with choosing a date other than the conventional one. They include:

1. Smaller crowds.
2. Frequent-flyer airplane tickets can be enjoyed without having to worry about the holiday black-out dates.
3. Christmas Eve and Christmas Day are free of hectic distractions and available for reflection, relaxation and enjoyment without pressure.
4. The opportunity to "clone" Christmas or Hanukkah. If it is so wonderful, why not celebrate it several times during the month of December?!
5. A date-free holiday. Sometimes we can dispense with the whole idea of having to choose a specific date and just enjoy the entire month as it is.

Once we have selected the most positive way to schedule them, then we can begin to plan the ways we will celebrate the holidays. Emphasize the fun of the unconventional approach, of having the power to break out of the mold if the mold doesn't work anymore. There are many, many options for making what once was a predictable routine into a memorable change of pace.

I will never forget the first time we celebrated Christmas following my divorce. I simply packed the kids into my old car, my son brought along a very small artificial tree and we had Christmas every night in a Holiday Inn on our way down to experience Disney World as a changed family. It was a very special Christmas — no presents — because we were saving our money for Disney World. However, I think that this Christmas stands out in the memory of my children as one of the best holidays they ever had.

Sometimes unusual company for Christmas puts a delightful spin on the season. I remember one Christmas we went to a local church and asked them to recommend a lonely family for us to share with. Not only did we enjoy the day but we had the good feeling of knowing that we helped somebody else have fun, too.

A good friend of mine chose a similar but different route. She took her entire family to a soup kitchen where everyone spent the day bringing small Christmas gifts to people at the shelter. They also participated in Christmas meal-making for others less fortunate than themselves.

Another family I knew simply could not face their big house that had always been decorated in high Christmas style. So the week before Christmas they loaded their car and took a cross-country trip, experiencing Christmas in many little towns across the United States.

A childless divorced woman I knew dreaded the Christmas holidays. She feared the loneliness and the emptiness of days when everyone else seemed to be having family fun. About a week before one Christmas, she decided she would expand her knowledge about different spiritual beliefs. From a Sunday paper she clipped out information on the services of various denominations. She went to church dinners, church sales, church services and church Christmas programs. She also checked out synagogues. By the time the season ended, she had made several potential new friends. She had found many people just like herself who were looking for something meaningful to do for the holidays. She was invited to several dinner parties and declared that year to be one of the best seasons she'd ever had. She was quite astonished that her first Christmas after her divorce could be so fulfilling and joyful. In the process, she also met a woman who became a close friend, and later a vacation companion.

George was very concerned about his children becoming melancholy over sad regrets as their first predivorce holiday season approached. So he and his children decided to keep their heads busy with games. He bought *Scrabble*,

Outburst, Trivial Pursuit, the old game *Twister, Bridge for Two* and *Personal Preference.* These were guaranteed to occupy them happily for the four or five days over the holidays when they would be together. Each night, prizes were passed out, small gifts that diffused the memory-loaded custom of opening gifts on Christmas Eve.

They invented another twist to the season by jointly preparing a different ethnic meal each night. There were Mexican dishes, Italian dishes and a German "festival." Everyone was surprised that their first holiday as a two-house family passed so happily and peacefully.

> *Holidays challenge us either to* live in the loss *or* grow from the loss. *Major changes always involve some loss but always present opportunities for positive, exciting choice-making.*

Traditional days for celebrating remind us that we need to be realistic about our losses. We can't suspend the grieving process just because it's Thanksgiving, Christmas or Hanukkah. But we can add positives to it. All of us who have read the work of Elisabeth Kubler-Ross and recognized the stages of grieving, have come to understand that we first have to face the loss and then the feelings about those losses, not bury them. Only then can we get busy and do something about them.

Since we know the first year following a divorce is likely to be difficult every time we approach a nostalgic date, we can allow ourselves to feel the negatives, *but* refuse to drown in them. For a full year we have to put a special effort into remodeling each holiday to disarm traditional flashpoints for melancholic moods. During the second year holidays will be noticeably easier, and with each subsequent year there will be less need to see the present in terms of the past. The ease with which we accept change will depend a great deal on how we handle that first year of grieving. So it becomes important to sit down with a calendar and review the special occasions that require a new look.

In addition to national holidays, each family has its own unique celebrations and annual events that need to be addressed. Maybe it's a special time of the year we spent with grandparents or an aunt. Perhaps it's the first trip to the beach at the beginning of summer or maybe the opening of ski season. If there is a child graduating from school, a wedding for one of the children from the family or even an annual garage sale that was the focus of family fun, you may want to invent ways to alter the occasion, making it newer in feeling. This doesn't mean you'll have to be "Special Events Director" for the rest of your life! — just for the first year, for both you and the children. After that, adjustments to each of these occasions will have been seen as fun, and the present will most likely be perceived as having more interesting possibilities than the past.

Many studies have shown that families that carry on traditions and routines but adjust them to a changing lifestyle are much better off when patterns in life are interrupted.

POSITIVES FOR KIDS WITH DIVORCED PARENTS

Professionals who work with families and children aren't really sure whether the difficulties experienced by "children of divorce" come from the divorce itself or from the years of struggle within the family, subsequent to divorce. While undeniably there are negative economic and social changes that affect many families of divorce, there are also many ways of looking at life for children after Mom and Dad split up.

On the up-side is the greater independence many children acquire. The learning can be a very painful experience or a healthy level of increased responsibility. Either way, the child has a head start on coping and often outperforms others in adulthood because of this early training.

So here are ways of seeing negative circumstances in a positive light:

1. Children learn to be responsible for themselves.
2. Children learn some mastery over their environment.
3. Children see the value of relationships and later in life may be more willing to work on a marriage. They may learn to cherish and nurture relationships *more.*
4. According to one researcher, children under 12 who live with divorced mothers often do better on achievement tests and have fewer skill problems than kids in two-parent homes. No one knows exactly why this happens, but it may be that divorced moms give kids the leisure time formerly spent with spouses. Perhaps with less stress in the home, it is easier to concentrate on studies.
5. Another researcher discovered that teens living with fighting parents are 1½ times more likely to lie, bully and express anti-social behavior, in general, than kids of divorced parents.
6. Adults whose parents were divorced are arrested half as often as adults from intact homes. This doesn't mean they don't suffer, but this sort of information is interesting.
7. In some economic groups, children of divorced parents tend to visit more attractions such as museums, zoos, lakes and beaches, and are more well-traveled than intact-marriage kids. This is especially true if one parent sees the children less often and finds an outing a better springboard for conversation than watching TV. (Working Moms with custody, and no

or inadequate household help, may hope that Dad takes charge of the excursions.)

Healthy families have nothing to do with whether there are one or two parents in them.

SINGLE-PARENT FAMILIES CAN BE HEALTHY AND HAPPY

Two-parent families like to think they have a much better edge over divorced parents at producing well-adjusted children, but the facts show that Mom and Dad together can do just as much damage as good. Children's emotional health is formulated by what they learn about themselves and life from the attitude(s) and lifestyle(s) of their primary caretaker(s), whether it's one person or two.

Following are some characteristics of painful versus healthy family systems, discussed at length in my book *Choicemaking* (Health Communications, 1985). From these lists you can see that viewing good parenting in terms of the number of parents is a far cry from what actually goes into building a happy, secure home and a strong sense of self-worth in a child.

Painful Family Systems That Lower Self-Worth Have . . .	**Health Family Systems That Build Self-Worth Have . . .**
A no-talk rule.	Open communication.
Internalized feelings.	Openly expressed feelings.
Unspoken expectations.	Explicit rules.
Entangled relationships.	Respect for individuality.
Manipulation and control.	Freedom that is valued.
A chaotic value system.	A consistent value system.
Rigid attitudes.	Open-mindedness.
Static traditions.	Flexible traditions.

A grim atmosphere.	A pleasant atmosphere.
Frequent chronic illness.	Healthy people.
Deeply dependent relationships.	Independent and growing relationships.
Jealousy and suspicion.	Trust and love.

Obviously painful families promote inadequacy in their family members. There are families with two parents in which alcoholic fathers frighten and intimidate their children; two-parent families where anger and hatred explode into physical and emotional abuse, sometimes with no intervention by the passive partner; two-parent families in which no one trusts the other, and lying and cheating are normal and expected. There are families where one or both of the parents spend so much time away from home that their children couldn't possibly develop emotional security, friendships or a sense of belonging. Often very troubled families think they are giving their children a decent home.

Then there are the families where there is peace, unity, respect and interest in one another. These homes are safe places to live, and children feel they belong. Whether these families have one parent or two, the result of a wholesome attitude and lifestyle is the same in the children.

The main effect of a reduction of the number of parents in a family is the loss of a helpmate in task-sharing. Time becomes more at a premium and children may have to reduce play time to work together with their parent on tasks. If this task assignment is done in a spirit of facing the challenge together and making more time for Mom to do those things that children want done for them, self-esteem can be enhanced, along with a sense of belonging and sharing in a safe and nurturing environment.

> *The messages in a troubled home are not clear.*
> *A divorce is clear and children can recover from*
> *it. Positively invite them to be new home builders*
> *with you.*

HOW OUR FAMILY SYSTEM DEVELOPED

People develop communication patterns that tend to protect their self-worth. We seek whatever pattern of communication best protects us in our system in terms of the personality we begin to develop. People learn their survival patterns in the families from which they come. They take this learning with them in choosing their mates and in raising their own children.

Many things are a matter of choice, but many aren't. The educational system today has an elaborate set of schedules, learning techniques and experiences which are enforced on students. The hope is that the student will learn to make "free" choices independently, yet that freedom has already been curbed to some extent by unchosen circumstances. When and where we are born, and which parents we are born to, are not matters of choice. A person enters the world "already begun," a unique personality yet needing to belong and needing to survive physically and emotionally. Maturity brings a shift from the yearning to be included to the desire to state, "I belong." While we do "our thing" and live in a certain way, we enjoy the discovery that we are important just for ourselves. The shift to one's "I-ness" is the process of growing self-worth. As the poet says in *Desiderata*, "I have a right to be here." A person in any family needs to be able to say, "I am important just because I am."

You can build this kind of family system and self-esteem among children on a daily basis, regardless of the number of parents in your family.

> ❧
> *As we let go of our fantasies of "happily ever after" and the myth of being a "perfect" family, we prepare ourselves and our children for meaningful partnerships and relationships in the "real" world.*

DEVELOPING A NEW FAMILY SYSTEM

How do you create a new way of doing things following a divorce? When healthy families communicate, people pick up on nonverbal messages and ask questions. Cliches such as, "Yes, dear, that's very nice" are nonexistent. Often families that are overly polite with one another are very troubled. But a postdivorce family that is trying to learn how to communicate will listen very carefully to one another. Even difficult emotions such as anger will be allowed. Anger will be aired, rather than allowed to fester.

In times of need, recovering families will be able to show what they are made of. They will be there for each other; no one has to be the sole hurting one. Everyone will be treated in the same way.

One characteristic of strong families — whether they're one- or two-parent — is to face problems early and be willing to solve them. Weaker families try to deny that problems exist or get into long battles over them, with accusations and blame. Their problems are not resolved and they only get worse.

When healthy families try to discuss problems, the focus remains on finding solutions. Painful families tend to focus on assigning blame. The ability to negotiate and compromise is the most important hallmark of a family. It is healthy to encourage your children to have different hobbies and sports and to like various foods, restaurants and movies. This kind of *different energy* can sometimes be celebrated by bringing the whole family together on a Friday or Saturday night and prompting everyone to share what has been meaningful to them that week. Two important dynamics occur when difference is promoted: One is that each child is validated for the beliefs, interests and styles they have, and secondly, everyone will learn from one another. This keeps a family energized and strong with each other.

A SOLID FAMILY CORE

All families, but especially divorced families, need to find a solidifying core that holds them together. In days gone by, very often that core was the nucleus of Mom and Dad. Sometimes it was a church. Today, as things have changed for many people, this core needs to be some kind of a value system. I know of one family in which the only factor that holds them together is the belief in individual respect for each person. Today, 12 years after divorce, the members still come together frequently. Even though the children are grown, the family meets four or five times a year because they know it's the one place, the one unit and the one group of people they can count on the respect their dignity, regardless of their accomplishments. They are always able to go home and receive validation for just being themselves.

Here is a list of ways to make a recovering, divorced family solid:

1. *Express appreciation often.* Look for opportunities to praise each other sincerely rather than pointing out annoyances.

2. *Ask the children to name the three favorite phrases they like hearing from the family.* Hopefully, they will be things like "I love you," "You can stay up late," "Yes, we'll order pizza," "Yes, we'll go to the beach (lake, mountains)." Be aware

that all families share some common pleasures and that supportive messages are important to them.

3. Build the self-worth and self-esteem of every family member every opportunity you get. It is so easy to tear esteem down and so hard to encourage it.

4. Promote different values among family members, such as different musical tastes, different hairstyles, different attitudes and senses of humor. Not only will this lessen the competition in the family, but it will bring members together to share their uniqueness and gain respect and honor for their differences. Differences, strangely enough, can become the core that holds the family together.

5. Teach everybody listening skills. At the family gatherings, every member needs a chance to talk for ten full minutes with no comment. During this time everyone can count on being heard without interruptions. Afterwards, you might want to close your eyes, take it all in, and then let the discussion go wherever it may.

6. Don't duck family problems. Face them with acknowledgment of feelings. Pull together the family members who have a problem. Allow each person a certain amount of time to share their feelings and their position. If the problem can be resolved, do it. If not, let it sit for a few days and try again. Don't be afraid to seek outside help if you need it. There are professionals around who can quickly help the family overcome the bumps of communication. Seeking advice sooner, rather than later, will help resolve the conflict with more ease and less pain a whole lot faster.

THE ORGANISM OF A FAMILY

A family is an organism with parts interdependent on each other. Its members operate in a system, as a productive whole whose parts work together for the common good. This system has a variety of goals: peace and harmony, efficiency and survival.

A family also resembles a mobile, one of those art forms made up of rods and string. Different shapes are hung on each piece of string. The beauty of the mobile is in its balance and movement. The mobile has a way of responding to changing circumstances like the wind or the touch of a hand. The mobile changes position, but always maintains balance. The whole system moves interdependently to maintain its equilibrium.

The beauty of the mobile is that even though the location of each part varies, that part still has its place and importance in the balance of the whole system. Each part is important to the balance of the whole, even though the shape changes. The mobile's movement towards balance is similar to a family's. As members go through life, families face the stressful circumstances of a new arrival, a tragic accident, an announcement of a serious illness or loss of a job. In response, family members shift to maintain equilibrium for peace, stability and survival.

A family system that works efficiently and effectively depends upon three factors:

1. Each family member must have an awareness of his worth and importance to the family.
2. The rules of living together support each other's self-worth, with respect.
3. Each family member must communicate congruently — consistently and honestly with himself and others.

In families of low self-worth, the members' fears and secrecies become paralyzing ingredients of the family stress. The members react to external behaviors, rather than respond to people. The goal of a dysfunctional family is not the nurturing of the members toward self-worth. In contrast, the goal is to rigidly maintain the pretense of family balance so that their identities as "wife," "husband" and "children of . . ." remain undisturbed.

LIFE-AFFIRMING ATTITUDES

With the confidence that is built on a peaceful family foundation, you and your children can center on life-affirming attitudes, such as the following:

- Having realistic expectations of yourselves and others.
- Appreciating your efforts and enjoying the support and compliments you receive.
- Taking some time each week for yourself, doing something that's important to you.
- Letting some events develop without controlling each move.
- Becoming increasingly aware of how you feel, and responding to those feelings.
- Affirming and appreciating those around you.
- Expecting wonderful things to happen to your children and you.
- Becoming increasingly pro-active.

Children can be shown that change is natural and not to be feared. In nature, we can observe that each season gives way to the next. Our children can learn to trust the changes in their lives and to observe that as one door closes, another opens.

DIVORCE WITH ADULT CHILDREN

Adult children and divorced parents frequently have a real need to establish boundaries. Adult children may have become enmeshed with one or both of the parents during the struggle of the marriage. Then when a divorce takes place, the adult child sometimes moves in as a surrogate partner. This is unhealthy for both child and parent.

Children and their parents should set limits and boundaries in their relationships, making sure each gets their primary needs met outside the parent/child relationship. This will allow their relationships to grow into a mature friendship.

Separating partners with adult children have many more options available to them. Each has the opportunity to develop relationships with the children that do not have to include as much contact with the ex-partner. Yet there may be times when partners' paths cross: graduations, marriages, crises and death.

A former couple has the best chance of handling these events without discord if they approach an occasion as two single people invited individually, like a sister and brother coming together because of a piece of past history. Focusing on this shared past, rather than on painful emotions as a former couple, is possible when we care enough about peace as a permanent part of our new family life.

9

A New You
For A
New Life

Joan: When there's alcohol in the family you grew up in, life is strange and you adjust. But that maladjustment can stay with you into a marriage where it doesn't make any sense and causes trouble. When I was a child, if I heard doors slam and furniture fall heavily to the floor or if I found my mother in tears on the couch, I pretended not to see or hear. The next morning, life would go on as if nothing had happened.

I learned not to say anything and I learned to worry. I was always trying to do what I could to help and at the same time feeling guilty for being a burden. I was angry because the other kids at school seemed so secure. I cried myself to sleep but I never told anyone. Daylight hours were for making people happy.

These reactions, year after year, became the
way I behaved when I had problems with
people. I never thought about how these
responses started or that everyone didn't react
as I did. To me this is what being a person was.
However, this way of dealing with life didn't
help my marriage.

Each time I went home, my father cried and
told me how much he loved me. After my first
child was born, we went home to visit but had
a horrible time. I could tell my father was
drinking constantly. He didn't look or act
drunk but he had that familiar glassy-eyed,
vacant look. For my own sanity, I had to leave
sooner than my parents expected. I knew the
only way would be to slip out with the baby at
night. But my father caught me and said that if
I left, I'd never be welcome again.

Later, whenever my parents called, I ran to
them. But it seemed as if I could never make
things right between them or for them. I felt
perpetually inadequate as I tried to help them,
but the alternative was to feel even more
guilty from not being there. Their house was
deteriorating, just like their lives and I wanted
to get involved in fixing it up. My husband
objected and said my energy should be spent
in *our* home with our children.

Then my parents started getting sick, one,
then the other. I would drive the 50 miles to
their home and rush back to take care of my
own family. It was taking too much out of me.
I was afraid my mother would die or that my
children would get hurt while I was gone. I
was worried I might get ill and "who would
take care of everyone then?"

As he tried to calm me down, I made my
husband feel helpless. Nothing he could say
would make the guilt or the worry about my
parents go away. I finally just collapsed, useful
to no one.

Part of my process of change included
professional counseling. It felt good to have
someone hear how I felt and to be reassured I
was a good person. I became able to separate
my behavior from who I was and separate the
disease of my parents from the people my
parents were. That's when I began to love and
respect myself in a new way. It was hard and it
took time, but it happened.

How could we have made such a mistake? Why did we
let "it" happen? What made us hang in there so long?

Maybe some of these questions have dogged you as
you've thought about the past. Also, what about the future? How can we possibly avoid future hazardous relationships when we didn't predict the crash of the last one?
Maybe we're stumped over why we held on so long to a
marriage that obviously wasn't made in Heaven.

Then there's what may seem to be the "Big Black Hole
of Singlehood" ahead. Maybe we're anticipating major
loneliness. Perhaps we've never really lived alone for long,
or were never good at it. Now we're by ourselves again
and we wonder how Sally or Jim can stand living alone.
What does it take not to go bananas, being the only adult
in the house?

EXPLORING THE PAST

After a marriage ends these two sets of self-doublts are
to be expected: "What's wrong with me that this divorce
happened (or this marriage happened at all)?" and "How
can I keep from feeling down about being by myself?" The

more you explore these doubts, rather than trying to bury them, the stronger you will emerge from postdivorce recovery.

> *The sooner you figure out your stumbling blocks, the better all your future relationships will be including the all-important one: you with yourself.*

Many of the painful feelings of divorce, and new efforts to avoid past mistakes, are complicated by deeply embedded programming, coming from our own families, our families of origin. A lot of us have not yet made this connection because what's not so comfortable in our relations with Mom, Dad and family seems "normal." The "glitches" in our family of origin are deeply familiar and we may feel, by the time we've been married and away for some time, that we pretty much have adjusted to them. This is especially true if home is far away or one parent or both have died. However, "out of sight, out of mind" doesn't apply with emotional issues. If we are having prolonged adjustment and grief problems associated with divorce and if we are concerned about not bringing old problems into new friendships, the prime suspect is our innocent maladaption to unresolved family issues.

Before we move forward in our new divorced state, it may very well help us to go backwards, to the root of why we have trouble giving up choices that hurt us and why we may feel insufficient or uncomfortable alone, unable to create our own happiness.

Detaching from the old, the traditional, the safe and familiar can cause various emotional reactions in people, ranging from disappointment or temporary regret, to sadness, depression, great hurt or panic. Most of us find it difficult to detach from a career, an organization, an institution or a family we felt good about. The degree of discomfort we feel clues us in to the depth of our problems with change.

If we are torn apart by our detachment, and we stay that way for too long, we may need to do some inner work on our relationships with our original family. The secrets to the way we react today may lie in the history of coping with our family of origin.

WHAT IS FAMILY DECATHEXIS?

Cathexis is a word taken from the Greek, *kathexis*. It implies holding on to a person, thing or idea. *Decathexis* is the process of breaking free.

I have to thank my husband, Joseph R. Cruse, M.D., for letting me incorporate some of his work into this section. He has helped many family members in their healing and growing process by introducing them to the concept of family decathexis, which is very relevant to the divorcing spouse and the changing family.

In divorce the job ahead of us is unhooking and becoming free of the ties that bind us to habitually destructive emotions and reactions. By discovering how we as children lost our free and unfettered sense of self, we will be able to reclaim the joy of an independent choicemaker. We will be able to move into new areas, new relationships and new levels of dealing with our spirituality, and improve our day-to-day living. As a result, you may find yourself way ahead of your predivorce self in your capacity to make good decisions, avoid harmful friends, develop your abilities and enjoy life.

It is natural when we lose our mates to feel that something is missing, that we are at a loss. Our spouses provided qualities that we may have lacked. They may have confirmed our worth by laughing at our jokes, seeking our opinion and sometimes even acting on it. At least part of their patterns of living — from eating to recreation, and maybe even religious practice — became ours. Now that's gone, and before the gap closes completely, we're going to continue hurting from the separation.

If our attachments have been extreme and intense, serving as our major drive and our means of identification, we are in real trouble when we lose them. The pain of loss lasts and lasts. It may turn into bitterness, fear of intimacy, fear of experimentation. In this way, our sense of feeling worthwhile is scrambled. It is as if we have become "cathected" — fixed. Literally, we are holding on for dear life. This response is not inevitable but something that arises spontaneously from a past in which guilt and fear figured prominently.

If we are having or if we have *always* had problems in letting go of people, places and circumstances, let's go back to our family of origin to see if that's where we learned to be dependent on circumstances for our wholeness and happiness. What about strong pressures to respond to our family's emotional needs? Were we made to feel guilty — either in a subtle or overt way — when we tried to separate or go our own way? At family reunions do we slide into roles that don't feel good just to keep the peace? Do we have a different *persona*, a different way of relating to the family, that doesn't feel natural and isn't like we are with friends?

When your behavior with family is substantially different and you feel like a kid when you go home, you should consider putting family decathexis on your agenda of important goals to strive for now that you're rebuilding your life. The process of decathexis not only realigns you in terms of reality with your family but it brings a latent strength up from your center that gives you the power to triumph over change in your life. It marks your real entry into adulthood — a state of living most characterized by being independent, not just by being over 21. You became independent of person or circumstance, capable of "making it" emotionally in this world.

> *Decathexis from family members, and subsequently from ex-spouses, does not mean detaching from loving them. It is, however, our resigning from participation in unhealthy family needs. This act of self-confirmation will empower our divorce recovery.*

SHAKING THE FAMILY TREE

Maybe we've tried to perform minor surgery on our relationships with relatives, but the results were either ineffective or only partially successful. Yet what is the alternative? Most people certainly don't want to stop talking to Mom or Dad or both altogether, and it's impossible not to think about their impact on our lives from time to time. But not needing their approval, saying no when we want to, confirming in our own minds our independence through affirmative interaction with them, may still be issues that we need to analyze and work on.

It's not enough just telling yourself you're an adult, and then falling in line when Mom or Dad "do their controlling thing." Your true self-appraisal is in how you allow yourself to be treated or, if your parents are no longer alive, what memories survive of your self-esteem in their presence.

Resolving the reality of your adulthood between you and your parents will go a long way towards healing the dependence and doubts about inadequacy in your post-divorce recovery process. Most of us choose to minimize the need to persistently deflect our parents' denials of our adulthood. We achieved some success in adolescence and don't want to relive that conflict or disrupt the truce we may have brought about since then. Moms are just that way, we say.

In a Sunday magazine story *(Tropic, Miami Herald, April 11, 1993)*, a foreign correspondent chuckled over her mother's embarrassing interference in her professional and personal life. In the story entitled, "A Fool and Her Mummy," the writer spoke of her mother's yearly April Fool's Day tricks as "true art." She wrote they are "aggressive," "proud" and "express as best she can her desire for an intimate connection — which surely is love, gritty and complicated as it may be." Her mother demonstrates, "She will not be excluded from my life," says the writer. After describing some of the practical jokes her mother had played, she made a statement which parallels the feelings so many of us have had:

> At this point, the reasonable reader must be wondering why I did not rage at my mother for crashing in on my professional life, for violating boundaries with impunity, for infantilizing me with my bosses. And in fact, I did rage. I did. But quietly. To myself. To my husband. Never to my mother. I was stopped there by habit, and by awe.

Whatever action it takes, serious attitude adjustment with your family is a prelude to enhancing your sense of can-do emotional maturity. It may be a daunting project. The alternative is continuing to hide from the possibility that long-term dependence is at the root of your sense of insecurity in crises. Healing from this dependency comes faster if we can take a close look at the whole process of becoming part of a family, then leaving it. The understanding that results in a foundation for understanding all the comings and goings of life.

Self-esteem cannot co-exist with dependency.

It takes action to break dependency. When dependency and parental expectations of a daughter or son become ingrained as ways to cope with family, plenty of confidence is needed to halt this response. The goal is not to change others but to act out your convictions for greater self-esteem. When we sacrifice our dignity or autonomy to keep the peace in the family, we are setting ourselves up for chronic inner conflict. In essence, we are giving ourselves the message that parents should be rewarded for having "brothered" with us by being allowed to exploit their parenthood status at our expense.

JUST WHO ARE WE?

This is a good question to tackle at identity-crisis times like divorce. We come into this world alone. We go out of it alone. Even before birth, our placenta which nourished us while our bodies were forming was only adjacent to the wall of the womb.

In fact, most of the time we're on this planet, we're alone, at least with our own thoughts. That does not mean we need to be lonely. We remain part of the family we're from and part of the family we've created. We all have duplicate pieces of our parents in us, and we can all see duplicate fragments of ourselves in our children. However, there is no other combination of organs, tissues, cells and *feelings* like us in the world.

You are unique, distinct — an individual. No matter how similar your outer body looks, you are still a different conglomeration of impulses and attitudes, driven in directions that can't possibly parallel your parents' paths. When someone says, "You look just like your Dad," there is a moment when we want to shout, "But I'm not him!" no matter how much we admire our Dad. Part of us senses that the danger of losing our identities is a real one. So much of our learning has been molded and modeled by our parents. However, we know that we are actually separate from any other individual who has existed before or will exist after us.

As infants we have an early and long history of dependence on others for our nurturing. But our family-of-origin's function is time-limited. The family as a place for parenting and "childing" has a specific lifespan, which is meant to dissolve its hierarchy after having served its purpose. A mother or father lion no longer wants to, or needs to, exert any authority over a former cub who is now grown to full size.

If it feels sad and difficult when you first think of claiming equality with your parents and of suspending your role in their eyes as a "child," then that's your signal, even stronger, for a need to apply decathexis. To become strong enough for durable relationships and to recover more quickly from personal setbacks in the future, you will need to act out this separation. To be able to consider ourselves self-contained, self-responsible and self-sufficient individuals, we need to expect, prepare for and perform a determined and joyful decathexis, or freeing, from the concept of a lifetime sentence as a member of just one family.

IF YOU'VE LOST YOUR PARENTS

When your first parent passed away, did you think, "Half of my parents are gone"? And when you lost the second parent, you may have realized, "I'm out here all by myself!" Regardless of your age, it often seems that the loss of the second parent results in a different feeling: Now we are totally separate. If our parents had been able to do a little better job of handling our independence to us all along, we might have reacted less like orphans and more like, "There goes another great friend: my Dad!"

Even if both your parents are gone, relating freely to yourself and others may be blocked by old messages of dependence. We take what we take from our families mostly because we have been caught up in the myth that they are the only reliable refuge in this world, no matter how inadequate. The reality that we can create our own refuge within, and maybe even a superior support system with friends, is a family heresy. But this is what true human maturity is about, and there are many parallels in nature. All mature creatures, both parents and offspring, go their own way, protect themselves, heal by themselves and make their own alliances. With humans, the difference is largely due to our ability to imagine more and subsequently, to fear more.

If you are having trouble trusting in your ability to recover and to live alone, don't underestimate the part played by society's conditioning toward dependence. Any guilt or sense of subservience you may still have stored in your family memory bank is a signal. Repeated challenges to your right to respond as you wish in family scenarios may have whittled down your self-esteem. Even more revealing was your coping method. Did you assert yourself but give in anyway? Did you swallow it in silence but keep coming back for more? Behavior patterns like these can be transferred to new relationships and undercut one's confidence in living alone.

"ING" ENDINGS DON'T FIT IN ADULT LIFE

When the time comes that parents shouldn't be "parenting" anymore, then children shouldn't be "childing" anymore. Why not make a verb out of the word *child*, too? Instead of being aggressive like parenting, it's a passive state of response tht is also widespread after adulthood. We hear the word "parenting" frequently but the word "childing" has not made dictionaries as yet. However, children learn very quickly what actions are expected of them as children, and all too often this role is later expected of them as adults.

Let's add that same "ing" ending to other family words and acknowledge them as the special verbs they have become. How about son? A person who is acting as a son is "sonning." A daughter acting out the expectations of a daughter is "daughtering." Some daughters act as daughters and some sons as sons long past the ages of 40, 50, 60 and even into their 70s. By acting as daughters and sons, we are not referring to the freely-given acts of love that one human naturally extends to any other cared-about person. We are referring to those disturbing words and acts that come as a response to an authority that should have ceased long ago.

Add the "ing" ending to the word "father." Now we're approaching a term longer in use, traditionally involving reproduction, period! But watch out! Here comes the block-buster . . . *mothering!* This is a very common word in our society, loaded with shades of meaning, both glorious and inglorious. For the most part, it is a well-understood and sacred concept. But why haven't the terms "daughtering" and "sonning" been invented and come to be equally revered? Maybe that would be too embarrassing an admission. Mother is overburdened, encouraged by society to cling and control; children are under-recognized for the psychological burdens they bear in this unnatural scheme of things.

We will always be daughter, son, mother and father, with histories we usually like to share. However, a verb side of our designations as relatives — the active participation in a sterotyped role that isn't natural after adulthood — needs to end for us to be free and powerful after divorce.

LETTING THE FAMILY ANCHOR SAIL

The belief that the family is the center of the universe can give us a measure of security while we're growing up and struggling to survive. Even if we grew up in a dysfunctional family, there may have been enough substance and enough need for love and connection to make us feel attached to whatever family member was available. But family attachment — which is not the same as love — after adulthood is the anchor that can't be lifted when we should be sailing away on our own.

If, instead of feeling glued into roles, children were encouraged to relate to their family members like friends after adulthood, life would feel much lighter for everyone. Imagine this conversation between a parent and child:

"Hey, one of these days, we're going to be loving adult friends and buddies. I will not parent you because you won't be a child any longer. Of course, you will always be my daughter (or son), but in addition, we'll be terrific friends with a long rack record of acceptance and tolerance."

Hard to picture? Doesn't sound quite right? A little *weird?* If so, that's because we have accepted the job of being someone's perennial child, a situation not conducive to reinforcing our self-esteem after a confidence-breaking divorce.

A HEALTHY FAMILY: TIME-LIMITED

The family — that is, a teaching, protecting unit — should be an active entity only while the child actually is lacking basic physical and social survival skills. Once children reach the age of 12 to 14, their ability to survive physically is fairly well in place. They probably could survive without further parenting and do, even at a younger age, in disadvantaged urban settings in developing countries. But social skills in today's complex society take longer to learn. This a the grey area in human evolution where society blurs its emotional needs with the needs of the children to develop self-confidence. At no time in life is social learning ever completely finished. Most of it is pursued long after the child leaves home.

Families need to change gears from tutors to friends as each child leaves home. To continue to chase the myth

that the "teachers" and "pupils" still exist and that there is
much to be owed and much to be paid, is a most destructive path arresting everyone's emotional and spiritual
growth. Many adult children, regardless of age and maturity, are still expected to be an active part of the family
until the youngest reaches majority.

> *Parents are not the only ones who may desire a
> lifetime of parenting. Many of us as adult children
> still attempt to resurrect our family of origin.
> True inner security develops only as we abandon
> this need as not natural.*

Family reunions are one way we may seek what we
have not yet developed in ourselves. These family "reu-
nitings" are fine if they are actually "old friends" getting
together for fun. But if they are plays of parenting and
childing, a place to try to get the acceptance and self-
validation we can't give ourselves or find in adult friends,
then they are stunting our emotional growth. Families
that have truly and joyfully decathected will still have
reunions but not occasions that attempt to recreate the
active family of the past. Spouses, young children and in-
laws will not be dragged to these events, only to feel shut
out by boring role-playing that is not part of their lives. A
healthy family get-together is not a commemoration of
dependency.

UNFINISHED ASSIGNMENT
OF PARENTING

The vast majority of parents never feel they've finished
their assignment as parents. They are threatened when
their offspring head out into the world, and they may
even feel guilt. Most of their self-worth may be wrapped
up in parenting and they may fear abandonment. Many

times we have heard parents say, "Boy, when all the kids are gone, we're going to really enjoy ourselves. Sure, we'll miss them, but . . . !" However, parents' feelings frequently don't match what they say. Underneath they are wondering about the loss of identity and status, loss of control and loss of companionship. Adult children soon discover the concerns. The conflicted reaction of the parents is normal and is passed down from generation to generation, even if it isn't verbalized. Some of the ways these feelings and fears are expressed might be through comments like:

- "What am I going to do after you're gone? (Said with a laugh.)
- "I've failed with that one, I guess!" (An aside to your aunt after you didn't show up for your cousin's wedding.)
- "I know you're 34, but you can always get your own apartment. We will only *be around* a little while longer!"
- "That hairstyle doesn't suit you."

FAMILY DEMANDS: AN ACCEPTED TYRANNY

Many families have spoken or unspoken expectations: "You're not coming home for Thanksgiving? Well, then, Mom probably won't bother making turkey and all the rest. I always looked forward to her great spread."

In the role of "second-class citizens," kids are just supposed to take this intimidation. Parents often aren't expected to consider the spouse's family or the young couple's right to start their own traditions. The unspoken focus is on "After all we've done for you . . ." In this way, childrearing in many families seems to be regarded as a debt that is never paid off.

Here's a familiar scenario: Daughter, bags packed, heads off to college, looking as though she's ready to do all that she's dreamed of, ready to set her own agenda, mark her own calendar with new people to meet and events to attend. But wait! She's already promised to drive the 300 miles back from school next weekend so Mom and Dad won't feel abandoned. Furthermore, she'll give up some new adventures to make that grueling trip time after time, whenever the guilt rises to uncomfortable levels. Sure, she wants to see them, but it's time she saw others, did things with others and learned about others. But there's no way Mom and Dad will discourage her visits back to the nest. She'll come back as a daughter who will jump into the process of daughtering, which means allowing herself to be mothered and fathered, advised and counseled, even after she protests it's not needed. She doesn't know how to stop the parenting without losing her parents. And she's been taught well to need parents permanently.

When she's married, the unnatural process will continue, only her husband will be drawn into it, either as a frustrated observer or in an active role, "sonning-in-law." By the time she's divorced, the parents may or may not still be on hand as havens of dependence or as voices from the past who remind her that she never quite outgrew her need for them. Daughters who have had a similar kind of parenting will have a difficult time recognizing that this binding, bonding and enmeshment, although normal, is not natural. Acceptance of what many daughters have to put up with indicates the lowered sense of self-esteem encouraged by family cathexis.

Sons caught in family webs have the same problem feeling strong and independent, despite outward appearances. They continue to undermine their own self-esteem by swallowing childing reminders from home such as "Support is always here if you need it," or, "Your mistakes might have been avoided by . . . (fill in the blank with your favorite family precautions)," or, "By the way, whatever happened to that nice girl who was interested in you during your senior year?"

As long as we are unable to assert the inappropriateness of being parented at our age, we are still feeling the need to be a child. This doesn't give us the strength we need in divorce recovery and definitely puts us at a disadvantage in a new relationship. A child can only handle relationships with friends or parents, not mates. Having the needs of a child and still wanting approval from a parent, an adult is too busy swallowing those emotional fishhooks of the family of origin to feel powerful and self-sufficient. Many times the line and the reel are represented by the telephone, as it becomes the mechanism to "reel us in."

DIVORCED CHILDREN OF DYSFUNCTIONAL FAMILIES

Adults who were raised in alcoholic or otherwise dysfunctional families face the same difficulties of those raised in "normal" families. But they have increased problems with trying to establish significant relationships, career paths and a life pattern that embodies self-worth. When we come from a family that is suppressed and emotionally dead, we don't decathect. We stay cathected. Instead of a separation into marriage or career, we simply part for a time. Then we go back and continue to try to fix up, console, support and be physically and emotionally vigilant and "on call."

If we're from one of these highly dysfunctional families, woe to the partner we chose. Usually our whole family is only too glad to incorporate themselves into our marriage, as if that had been the plan all along. A partner may have to fit into a set of rules, standards and traditions that can be quite rigid, especially for a new relationship that has just begun. When spouses find their beds must be shared with painful and unhealed family injuries, scars, complicated negotiations, power battles and "responsibilities," the marriage often becomes strained. This is because neither parents nor adult children could step off the societal "sad-go-round" to grab that golden ring of independence.

Declarations of independence aren't negations of love. Ex-spouses in divorce recovery may need to affirm their own powers by actively rejecting parents' traditional rights to emotional dependence.

Most often, people from dysfunctional families are attracted to potential partners who are also from families with serious problems. They have a lot to talk about. So it isn't just one spouse who will have to struggle with a "foreign" set of rules but two. This is double trouble for a marriage or relationship. When we have such an entourage with us, we find that we are seldom able to join in the life of someone we may meet who is full of choices, free and growing. Each day holds the excitement of free choice and positive self-regard for a "former child," without the encumbrances of a "cathetic family."

THE REALITIES OF PERSONHOOD

Yeah, you may say, but isn't this all very idealistic? Actually, no. What is idealistic is the image of the family and all the assumptions its members make. What is realistic is that when we are true to ourselves, and understand why anything else doesn't make sense, we don't hurt forever. We can withstand setbacks, such as a separation or a divorce. We can feel alone but not lonely. We can be honest with a new friend.

When adults and their parents go in for counseling together, such as in an alcohol treatment center, it is not approached by therapists as true "family therapy." That is because realism must prevail and the family hierarchy must be treated as obsolete. This kind of counseling is called "conjoint adult therapy." Family therapy involves kids who are still doing their childing and parents who are still doing their parenting. They are still an active family, subject to the needs of the parents as well as the children.

Once we are divorced, where do we put our energies in terms of our families? Who do we spend our time with? Where do we put our focus?

We need to focus on the reality at hand. If we insist on trying to retain or resurrect any of our previous family relationships, we will delay the opportunity for a full life. At the same time, if we have children, we are handing down the old message of adult child imprisonment in the family of origin.

LOVING WHILE CLAIMING OUR "RIGHTS OF PASSAGE"

Does decathexis mean that we will stop loving, seeing, enjoying or depending on one another? Absolutely not! After all, who else has more of an investment in relationship than mothers and fathers and sons and daughters and sisters and brothers? But let that relationship be what it is, if it is: the kind of great *adult* friendships that grow with age, experience and sharing as equals. Rather than only paying lip services to rites of passage, such as graduation and marriage, we need to actively assume the "rights of passage" and move on from our families of origin, taking with us our titles of son, daughter, mother or father, but leaving the active roles of sonning, daughtering, mothering or fathering behind.

"FAMILY FRIENDSHIPS"

When we are able to leave behind the active family roles of our childhood and move into "family friendships," we continue to nourish those friendships. We can treat them as real friendships that don't thrive on assumption

and duty. Without care and attention to these relationships, it is easy to fall back into the familiar "ing" way of
relating, creating discomfort, resentment and disagree-
ment. Being realistic, we need to be alert to the interac-
tions and dynamics within our family friendships, which
do not occur in our other close friendships.

COMPARISONS

What kinds of demands do you make of your best
friends? Do you make the same demands that you, as
parent or adult child, make of your children or your parents? Looking at that issue can be very enlightening.

Do we as parents or adult children treat one another as
we would our closest and dearest friends? Let's ask some
questions of ourselves regarding our friends and see if
the behaviors toward our parents and our children are
similar or identical. They should be, unless we have some
very close friends we're parenting or being parented by!

In other words, try answering the following questions
regarding your three closest friends — questions that
deal with parenting, "familying" and "childing" — and experience how unrealistic it is to attempt carrying out our
roles with other family members into adulthood. The first
set of questions are those dealing with parents, reflecting
common expectations from their adult children.

Would you expect your best friend to . . .

- Interrupt each weekend for a visit with you?
- Borrow money and not repay it?
- Drive or fly 1,800 miles to see you every vacation,
  Thanksgiving or Christmas?
- Need, want and accept advice every time you feel
  compelled to give it to them?
- Accept your requirements for the relationship with-
  out question and stay in a support role most of the
  time?

- Strive and sacrifice to meet educational, occupational, materialistic and social goals that you have set up for them?
- Follow in your footsteps and model after you?

Doesn't it sound slightly ridiculous in this perspective? Yet society says this ridiculous behavior is okay from parents, since childing creates a debt that can never be repaid with love alone. However, the only suitable sacrifice is the adult child's integrity. It's hard to feel qualified to stand on your own two feet when the foundation of your life is warped with this kind of conditioning.

Conversely, parents themselves may bear an unrealistic burden of expectations from their children when this continuity of role playing exists. The following questions might be used as a reality test by adult children who are still dependent on parents when gauging the appropriateness of their need.

Would you expect a friend to . . .

- Give you a loan on top of a loan?
- Babysit on the Friday of your choice?
- Have you to dinner every holiday?
- Give you their car whenever yours doesn't work?
- Let you drop in unannounced for lunch or dinner?
- Take your kids shopping for clothes at your request?
- Get one of your kids out of jail in the middle of the night?
- Let your kids walk on the furniture, play tag in their house or slide on varnished floors?
- Keep their refrigerator stocked for your kids to raid?
- Let your kids rifle through bureau drawers and ask for what they fancy?
- Let you store your stuff in their garage year after year?
- Put their needs as a couple secondary to yours as an individual?

Another unlikely set of behaviors to be found among friends is that of always checking in on, checking up on, reporting in to and reporting to one another (as both children or parents may feel is necessary). We're not talking about the fun closeness of best friends by anxious constant contact. Would a good friend who cares about me, respects my personal life and my independence cling or snoop like this? Would I do this to a friend?

UNCONDITIONAL LOVE AND TOTAL DECATHEXIS

The unconditional caring and love that occurs in friendships is rare among parents and their adult children. Individuation — becoming your own person — is a time for joy, for recognizing, feeling and celebrating your own maturity and personhood. Decathexis — a reality-based separation for purposes of freedom — is a hallmark of having made it as a human being. If we learn to decathect and to celebrate ourselves as separate, unique individuals, we can love and be loved by family members without the need to cling to a family when its "operating" time is over. Knowing that we are whole and complete within ourselves, we can move with candor, serenity and joy, in and out of our various families.

Many societies celebrate decathexis and perform a separation ceremony within the family unit. A majority of parents and their children in most societies, however, have accepted the subjective "rightness" of ignoring this need or of minimizing its importance. Even though we have bas and bar mitzvahs, graduations and weddings, we rarely let loose of our old roles. Indeed, there is often the need for reassurance that everything will stay the same, as the tears flow. ("My little girl! I can't believe she's graduating from college!")

If family members have not gone through decathexis when they physically left home, it still isn't too late. You can decathect from your parents when you're 28, 35 or

57. As a parent you can decathect from your adult children at any time. But late decathexis is a radical change from the enmeshed family pattern of expectations that has become a way of life. As a result, it can have its moments of pain and indecision.

Care and caution and full explanations to other family members may be necessary. Professional counseling would be useful in some very entangled families, and it is available if needed. The rewards of greater personal growth and self-esteem justify the effort and the investment.

The concept of unconditional love and total decathexis is well stated by Kahlil Gibran in *The Prophet:*

Your children are not your children.
They are the sons and daughters of
      life's longing for itself.
They come through you but not from you,
      and though they are with you,
      yet they belong not to you.
You may give them your love but not your thoughts,
      for they have their own thoughts.
You may house their bodies but not their souls,
      for their souls dwell in the House of Tomorrow,
      which you cannot visit,
      not even in your dreams.
You may strive to be like them,
      but seek not to make them like you.
For life goes not backward
      nor tarries with yesterday.
You are the bows from which your children
      as living arrows are sent forth.
The Archer sees the mark upon the path of the
      Infinite. And He bends you with His
      might that His arrows may go swift and far.
Let your bending in the Archer's hand
      be for gladness;

For even as He loves the arrow that flies,
so He loves also the bow that is stable.

COMMON FEELINGS

Following are some feelings that are remarkably common to both divorce trauma and family cathexis:

- *Hurt* is a catch-all expression but generally it's the result of feeling a loss of respect.
- *Anxiety* is the fear of being hurt or of losing something essential to one's happiness. Whether it is reality-based or not, it feels the same. It alerts us to defend ourselves.
- *Anger* is very often a response to being hurt. It is high-octane irritation and annoyance. Anger not resolved becomes rage.
- *Guilt* is the feeling of being unworthy or bad, or of being perceived as bad. It is repressed anger turned inward. It is being sorry about something you did or couldn't do. It is about a bad deed, while *shame* is feeling that you *are* the bad deed.

ACTUALIZING THE NEW YOU

Strength begins with self-ownership and pride that we act true to our feelings in our most important relationships. No one owns us, no matter what our relationship with them might be. We are not here on this planet to fulfill the unmet dreams of a parent or to protect another person from facing the reality of herself or himself in the world.

We do seem to be here to be ourselves and not someone else, to develop and grow, to be as honest and true to our real feelings as we possibly can dare. The tremendous diversity and uniqueness of individuals is the miracle of humanity — our *built-in* self-worth, just waiting to be appreciated. We crumble in crises like divorce only if we're talked into believing our worth is bestowed upon us by others. We can only make the world a better place to live if we first learn how to live our own lives freely.

What is it you want for yourself in this life? What are you doing to get it? What's in your way? Who put your stumbling blocks in place? Why have you waited for a crisis to force you to act?

These are tough questions to ask, but the process of answering them leads to emotional self-sufficiency and new, loving relationships. Tossing out the deadwood of family misconceptions takes a strong arm. But by carting around the burdens that aren't rightly yours for so long, you may have built up just the muscle you need. Now is the time for a good emotional workout. As we clear away the practical and emotional complications of our divorces and our family independence issues, each of us is able to discover that "I am worthwhile simply because *I am!*"

10

Dating, Sexuality And Remarriage

Joan: There were just too many problems unresolved from both my family and my first marriage, so my second marriage also fell apart. He was a nice man but the bulk of the finances was on my shoulders. After counseling we still got divorced because then we could clearly see that we just didn't mesh. I was single for a few years after this second divorce, but it wasn't the painful experience I had after my first marriage. I began seeing myself as a survivor instead of a bad person and a failure. I felt like a personal success story just to be raising my children to healthy adulthood.

After I became established professionally and knew what I could achieve, I felt like a complete person. I was actually enjoying the single life. My time alone was really very

important as I was becoming more mature.
Just when I figured I'd probably be alone for
the rest of my life — and could enjoy that —
along came my soulmate! I was now ready for
him. I could take as well as give, and give
freely, without feeling anything I did would be
inadequate.

When we married, it was like for the first
time. My other two marriages had to do with
fulfilling painful needs. This one was about
two independent people who understood
themselves coming together. Yes, we had to
negotiate and make compromises. But we were
able to do that. We were both strong and we
had both healed from our pasts.

Ken: I cannot believe I have made as many
choices, decisions and changes as I have in the
last 12 years. It's a separate life, in many ways.
I know I could live happily today being single,
but after some time I found a woman I just
had to ask to marry me. We had a lot of
difficulty in our early years together from my
children's resistance to her. They didn't want
me marrying anyone in general, and her,
especially.

For a long time I felt pulled between my
children who wanted me to return to their
mother, and the woman who loved me. I was
still in therapy when I remarried, and it finally
sank in that I had to be true to myself or no
one would ultimately be satisfied.

Kathy: I was so much more ready for
sharing my life with someone when I met my
second husband. Sharing children with two

families is nothing I could have handled before.
I wasn't even conscious of what intimacy,
relationship or responsibility were at the time
I married Jim.

Doyle and I now have a beautiful little child
of our own, Tommy, who is the full-time
resident. This causes some problems with my
two step-children. I have to reassure them that
Tommy is not any closer to us than they are,
just because he was born to both of us. I try
to make the stepchildren feel equally loved
and I treat them all the same way. I took a
chance with this marriage under these
circumstances and I give myself a lot of
credit for being able to make it work.

Bob: After my first marriage flopped, I
dated a lot. A real lot. I was almost afraid of
remarriage. There was no way I wanted to go
through the pain and bitterness again. But
after a while I thought less and less about
what had happened in terms of how it still
affected me. I was very cautious about getting
serious with a woman again, but I was also
feeling more confident about myself. I was not
the person who made that first mistake. By
the time I decided to marry Suzie I had really
done some soul-searching and had discarded a
lot of deadwood out of my system.

I can truthfully say I have never felt as much
trust and fulfillment with someone as I have in
my marriage today. Occasionally we have a
flare-up but we don't worry about those. We're
still two different people. I have a solid
relationship with my wife and I intend to
honor that at all costs.

Suzie has two kids and we have one together.
Everyone understands this is a team effort.
We never let the kids come between us. We
know they will grow up and leave, and we will
still be here together. My wife's a full partner
with me in all the decisions we make, about the
kids or otherwise. We are enjoying life.

THE PROSPECTS OF DATING AGAIN

One of the scariest features of divorce for many ex-
spouses can be the prospect of dating again. We sense that
something is different out there. We *know* we are different.
It's been a while since we were totally footloose with no
emotional ties, no promises or exclusive arrangements.
Suddenly we are part of a singles scene which, by the way,
seems to incude a lot of people younger than we are.

TAKE IT EASY AT FIRST

If this were a perfect world where no temptations
crossed our paths until we were ready to deal with them,
we could wait a year before seriously dating anyone. That's
what 83 percent of the ex-spouses I surveyed recommended. They pointed out that there are several personal
concerns that really should be ironed out before we're in
the best position to tackle a relationship that could get
serious. Some good reasons they felt ex-spouses should
take it easy with dating in the first year include the
probabilities that:

- We're still on an emotional roller-coaster.
- We're confused.
- We have a need for self-care.
- Multiple changes in our lives are taking up our atten-
  tion.
- We may be trying to re-order our priorities in life.
- Our family healing needs attention.
- Our financial changes may make a difference.

- Our work concerns may be all the extra pressure we can handle.

Relationships — even light-hearted ones — take time and energy. Most of the participants in my survey recommended socializing in groups, attending parties and dinners, but not yet getting emotionally involved with one person.

An interest in making new friends and an interest in dating are, of course, not the same. The person who is only looking for new friends is focused on *socializing*. The person who is looking for a mate is *dating* and needs to be prepared for the difference. Looking for friendships is a pleasure and socializing is fun. If you are focused on finding a new partner, add the elements of excitement, but also concern. Then you may feel some pressure to be and look your best and to evaluate more critically the person you are with.

Do you need the extra complications of dating right now, as welcome and ego-boosting a distraction as it may be? If you just want to socialize, you can ask people over. If you're angling for a serious relationship, then you may feel it necessary to take the traditional stance of waiting to be asked out. This imposes its own limits and probably adds frustrations to your efforts to build a new circle of friends. Learning to enjoy your own company and casual socializing first, helps build a stronger foundation for a possible future partnership.

Premature dating after divorce can lead to regrets that you weren't fully ready for a new relationship. Casual socializing gives you more time to get used to yourself as single.

As the months go by and healing takes place, you will feel the confidence in your new identity rising. This is the ideal time to enjoy your single status and take on the "response-ability" of dating relationships or another coupleship.

WAYS TO MEET A NEW PARTNER

They are endless, but in case you've forgotten:

1. Wear or carry a conversation piece — a book, an unusual unbrella, a piece of jewelry, a small dog (doubles as protection!).
2. Find out what makes you feel more desirable. Whether it's a neat pair of lucky suspenders, a silk shirt or lingerie by *Victoria's Secret*, when you feel desirable, you will come across as more desirable.
3. Tell your friends that you are dating.
4. Take a singles' vacation. There are all kinds of singles' trips that are often put together around particular activities, such as deep sea fishing, camping, photography or hiking. You might not only meet someone, but you'll have a good time while you are doing it.

COUPLESHIP AND REMARRIAGE IN THE '90s

Chances are that you'll find relations in the 1990s aren't much similar to relationships in the '80s or '70s, not to mention the '60s. Back in the '60s and through much of the '70s, the sexual revolution was in full swing. Sex had a very high priority in relationships.

By the '80s, many couples were running out of steam. Lack of desire rapidly became the number one sexual complaint, and it continues to be a concern in the '90s. The economy, high personal debt levels and job burnout are part of the problem as layoffs and cutbacks force more work into the hands of fewer people. Also, many people in the '80s had a more specific commitment to their jobs — and to their fitness club — than they had to one another.

After scrambling to get too much done at work, couples then tried to wedge intimacy, closeness, emotional fulfillment and sex into, maybe, the half-hour between 11 and 11:30 at night. There is also concern and necessary fear surrounding AIDS.

Couples aren't necessarily suffering from dysfunctional sexual lives, but may be suffering from dysfunctional lifestyles.

Maybe the good news about couples' down-shifting from the sexual revolution is that people are beginning to find there's more to partnering, more to relationships and more to life than sex-in-overdrive. Sometimes sexual enjoyment is still a high-priority item, but there's more tolerance now for an ebb and flow that acknowledges additional commitments of our energies. Just because other interests are taking priority doesn't mean that love is out the window.

As you begin dating, you may well find that sexual norms have changed from your pre-marriage days. Rather than finding people who know all there is to know about the mechanics of sex, you may encounter more who are looking for a relationship that emphasizes the whole person. They don't want to work so hard at being sexual. Relaxation, conversation, touch, hugs — more of a whole body experience with one another is popular. With this comes more complete intimacy — a surprise to many who felt they had to work for it — and more sexual satisfaction. Sex today tends to go beyond the climax-oriented sex of the '60s and '70s to a physical relationship that bonds body, mind, heart and spirit.

TUNING IN

Despite all that's been written in magazines, newspapers and books about being close and being sexual, I've found many couples continuing to enter a relationship or partnership without the foggiest notion of what togetherness is all about. In my book *Intimacy And Sexuality* (ON-SITE Training and Consulting, Inc., 2820 West Main St., Rapid City, SD 57702; 1991), much can be found about the understanding of couples that I obtained during my years as a marriage and family therapist. If you want to get back on track with touch as a means of communication, you might want to review some of the areas that bogged you down and were not working in your marriage.

Communicating at various levels is often a problem. When couples with marriage difficulties come to me and say, "We have problems with communication," it almost always translates to, "We can't talk about our sexual relationship. We talk around it, as we do around our other kinds of blocks."

The first step in solving a communications problem with someone else is to solve it with yourself. Many of us can't even communicate our needs to ourselves. We may hide from one feeling to gratify another. But if you can't have an honest relationship with yourself, it's even harder to have one with someone else. By pulling out *all* the feelings, including the contradictory ones, and sharing them with yourself, and then others, a full picture of a real loveable person will emerge.

We have many, many feelings every single day, yet most of us only talk about a few: *mad, sad, guilty, hurt* and *ashamed.* All the rest are actually the language of intimacy, the ones that explain the others. Be fully aware of how you think, what you feel and how you behave, then work on the ability to share that with another.

PASS THE PASSION

The capacity to share our feelings is the basis of the word "passion." Check out its meaning in the dictionary and you may be surprised.

Passion *means "full of feeling,"* not just lust or excitement. *Being passionate is being yourself, freed of the emotion-blocking burdens of the past.*

You can increase your passion potential by taking the time to feel aspects of life you might have been missing. I know that I've experienced passion at seeing beautiful sunsets, experiencing natural childbirth, being a part of the birth of my grandchildren and by listening to some fantastic music. That, to me, brings about thoroughly passionate feelings on a par with sexual enjoyment. Narrowing our passionate expectations to just one area of expressions stunts us. Listening to great music, we can not only hear it but expand our sensory appreciation to feel it with our entire bodies. Opening ourselves to a fuller range of feelings helps us open up the others and experience them on a deeper level.

When we *feel* our feelings, not only observe them, we release ourselves to more passion. This means we have to admit the painful feelings, too — agony, despair and loss — acknowledging both ends of the spectrum, from ecstacy to despair. We can't improve our passion potential by editing out the feelings we'd rather not have. Passion is about fullness, not about holding back.

To develop the capacity to enjoy a rich relationship with someone special, we can exercise our feelings by having a full-body experience with people we meet. When you are close to someone, practice your awareness of what they project. Our energy fields extend about three feet around us and can send messages as clear as "I'm angry," "I'm at ease," and even "I'm not tuned into anything!"

Blending is the process that happens when we feel our own passion and another's, when we are able to express our feelings and find they tune into the same frequency as our partners. You can trust blending as a safe experience when you can trust yourself to feel more fully.

TRUST AND SAFETY FIRST

Healthy people don't just walk up and expose their deeper feelings to any willing listener. Correspondingly, emotionally sound people don't do this with their bodies, either. Most of the time, after feelings of safety and trust have been proven sound, some kind of commitment develops: to care for each other, to be honest with each other and to nourish one another. As we become closer, this commitment increases the flow of passion.

Figure 10.1. Holding Hands

EMOTIONAL INTERCOURSE AND TRUST

A bonding of feelings is what everybody seems to want but it just doesn't happen with physical or mechanical intercourse. People can have a lot of sexual activity and yet say, "I still feel so empty! I still feel so lonely!" Their hunger is a lack of intimacy, an unfulfilled need to be vulnerable with another person and to know that they're safe in this relationship of trust. There is a commitment to care about each other. When that happens, two people are able to use their sensory systems to move from sharing and intimacy into emotional intercourse. Then a truly full, physical intercourse occurs that mirrors the mutually satisfying emotional sharing that is underway.

> *When two people are able to share their feelings in an atmosphere of safety and trust, they are enjoying* real intimacy *or emotional intercourse.*

Sometimes the recently divorced, who are still caught up in feelings of betrayal, have trouble trusting a new lover. As a result, sexual enjoyment may be fleeting. When the betrayal issue is worked out, we learn to trust ourselves again because of the understanding we've gained. We stop attaching negative expectations to members of the opposite sex just because of our former spouse's behavior. When we understand what went wrong with our previous marriage, we put ourselves in a position to trust ourselves and others.

FOCUSING ON OUR SEXUALITY

Trust is necessary to maximize our use of *sensate focus*. If we are worrying about our new partner also betraying us, we cannot focus on sexual enjoyment. Our sensory system is sidetracked. When our sensory system is fully attuned, there is this faculty available to us called sensate focus. It enables us to concentrate on any part of ourselves and make it work for us. If you want to focus on a sight, a sound or a smell, you can with this power.

When we are interested in achieving sexual enjoyment, we direct sensate focus to the genitals. If we are feeling safety, trust and commitment, and are feeling very good about the intimacy that we have with someone else, we have the ability to sensate focus on our genitals and

become physically aroused consistently, not just the first
few times.

When we are aware of both these two elements necessary for continued sexual enjoyment, we see that we,
ourselves, play an important part in our own pleasuring.

*It is not just the other person's responsibility to
arouse us. Our minds and hearts must be centered
on our capacity to respond.*

We, ourselves, have to bring sensate focus to the relationship and have as a partner someone with whom we
feel so safe that this focus is easy. Every female, therefore,
has the responsibility to bring about the conditions for
her own arousal. Every male has the responsibility to
bring about the conditions for his own arousal.

When each person has taken the responsibility for her
or his own arousal system there is an emotional and physical consequence, otherwise known as an orgasm, a full-
body orgasm. This is not just a mechanical high, since it
can be felt in the fingertips, in the toes, in the entire body,
as well as the genitals. With that, often comes an emotional high which is equally satisfying and pleasurable.

Often in relationships that aren't quite *right*, an orgasm
is followed by an abrupt sense of separation. Although
we'd burn out if a climax didn't end sometime, partners,
in a relationship of trust and love return to where they
started from after an orgasm, into an atmosphere of intimacy and a feeling of safety, trust and commitment. And
when this happens, they are then able to move into what
I call *emotional afterplay.*

Emotional Afterplay

The first 20 or 30 minutes following intercourse that
results in climax is a highly sensitized time. We are

sensitized physically and we are sensitized emotionally. It is a time that can be best used to create further bonding and trust for the couple. This can be done by:

- Sharing more with each other.
- Telling each other something very personal.
- Letting the other know of the love you feel.

What a wonderful bonding time — there's none better! Let's tell our partners how much we care about them and what they mean to us. Affirm the person's specialness. A speech isn't necessary, just a few heartfelt words. As a relationship progresses and people get more and more comfortable with this kind of sharing after intercourse, they can make it a fun time. They can be silly with each other. They can play with the other's child within. They can laugh and have a good time, just like two little children who are able to enjoy one another without pretense or rules.

Figure 10.2. Heart

Each experience of trust and joy, along with the bonding of affirmation, is one that cements commitment and nourishes love. It helps people retain and build on their ability to be passionate. It is a wonderful truism that the longer a couple has intercourse in real intimacy, affirming of one

another's worth, the more passionate they become. The
older they get and the longer they are in a committed
relationship, the more their fullness of feeling stays full.

> *Passion based on caring and trust doesn't di-
> minish with age or time. The opposite happens:
> Each passionate experience is a coin that adds to
> our sexual wealth.*

SEXUAL RELATIONSHIPS THAT AREN'T SAFE

It's hardly unusual to find people having sexual relationships with partners they barely know, much less trust.
Seductions, affairs and short-term contacts are common
not only because people are interested in becoming close
to someone, but also because these relationships are new,
exciting, possibly secretive, and they make us feel intensely, even if briefly. They are an easy fix with no personal investment necessary. They require no previous commitment to ourselves, no self-understanding, no "other"
understanding. However, many people find that as soon
as familiarity sets in — guess what? The connection
doesn't excite anymore. It's all external, nothing to do
with anything real and lasting.

The unworkability of these relationships may be smoth-
ered in impossibly idealistic fantasies, of romance: "She is
exquisitely sensitive!" or emotional stimulation due to dangerous circumstances: "Her husband sits behind me at
work!" or their novelty: "He's a race driver!" or sheer
physical attractiveness: "He is 6'2" and looks like a Greek
god!" Sometimes the fact that the person is totally unknown is the prime stimulation: "I just met this person
and she really turns me on!"

The Trap Of Novelty Romances

All these novelty feelings may make those whose lives

are sluggish feel vibrantly alive so that their sensate focus can be activated. But the focus remains only as long as the emotional newness of it survives. This syndrome is so frustrating and so filled with shame as we move on from person to person to person in order to feel *something*.

People may seek short-term relationships for a number of reasons. Their past may include emotional trauma in which trust has been broken, commitment has been betrayed, and closeness brought hurt and emotional pain. Closeness no longer feels safe.

SHUTDOWNS

We can also be shut down because of sexual abuse or emotion "medicators" like alcohol, drugs and nicotine. Nicotine and cocaine are very powerful repressors of emotions. Workaholism and food disorders also repress feelings. There are many medicators, some behavioral and some chemical. All of them work in the same way, making our feelings unavailable to us. Even constant busyness, frenetic activity, excessive exercising and body building can put a cap on the feelings that contribute to intimacy.

MECHANICAL SEX

Mechanical sex is sex that takes place outside of a person's emotional range. The stimulus for arousal comes from our minds, even though a sense of lack may prompt the need. If we have shut down from physical or emotional medicators, we have to rely on artificial stimulation in order to become aroused. The most frequent artificial stimulations are chronic masturbation, pornography, affairs, seductions, violence and danger, (i.e., living on the edge).

The partner of someone involved in mechanical stimulation naturally finds sex much less satisfying. One reason is that it is the norm for men to be able to be stimulated faster, most of the time, than females. When one person reaches climax before the other (who may feel either angry, hurt or left out), there is no way for them to become

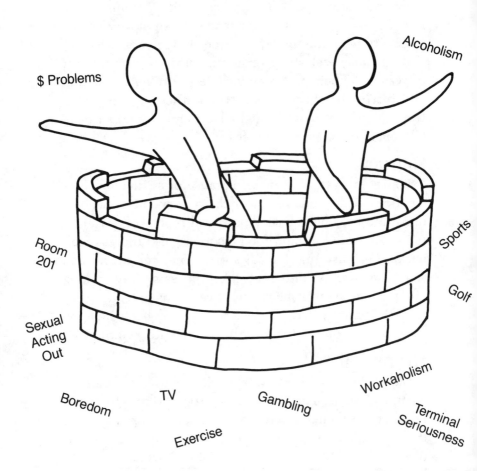

Figure 10.3. Medicators

really fulfilled. Certainly not emotionally. Even sex between two people, without emotional intercourse, is not much more than masturbation. Climax becomes a mere product, a physical release, period!

Then comes a letdown. When there was no intimacy to begin with, the letdown is often painful. The relationship may have started out as two people with parallel desires to somehow connect, but they were never able to share their feelings and build anything more than a limited intimacy. Their sexual coupling is dependent on artificial stimulation. After climax, their feelings head downhill. Both people may begin to feel a certain sense of discomfort. Here you are in a very close, intimate place with another person, and you have no idea how that person is really feeling about you. There was no talk about feelings (other than sexual) before, and there's none now. It's a place that doesn't feel good, except if you have determined it's better than having to face your problems with intimacy.

VIOLENT "LOVERS"

There is another kind of dysfunctional relationship that is both exciting and dangerous enough to stimulate emotional bonding for some people. The arguing couple who suddenly become "love birds" is often symptomatic of people who need a powerful fight to arouse their sense of connectness. Only when the other has screamed loudly enough to show "caring" can their sensate focus really kick in. Perhaps they had parents who set this pattern as "normal" and weren't able to create much self-esteem in their youngsters. Unfortunately, a relationship like this can go on indefinitely. But who would want it to?

SEXUAL ATROPHY: A PATTERN FROM THE PAST?

A recent study showed that the single most common sexual problem reported to marriage counselors by couples in the United States was a lack of desire. "Too busy" or "not interested" were frequent responses. After a

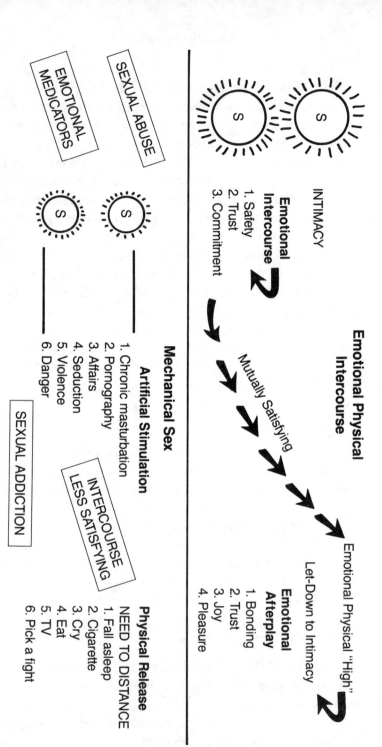

Figure 10.4. Sex

while, people adjust to almost anything, including something so basic as sex or lack of it. They develop a sort of comfortable arrangement in which there is silent agreement not to even talk about it anymore. Then one partner notices that two months have passed since any intimacy. Three months have gone by. Six months have gone by. A year has passed since there has been any kind of passionate connection. The reason behind the indifference may be so painful that eventually closeness is avoided altogether.

Divorced partners may have built up a negative response to sexual contact, based on a long time of avoiding a problem partner. If this is you, give yourself a chance to break the momentum of avoidance or apathy. Negative habits can take a while to deprogram from our system, just as they took some time to become established.

SEXUAL RECOVERY

One person cannot have a meaningful relationship for two. Both people need to make whatever commitment for trust and safety is necessary in order for them to broaden their understanding and enjoyment of each other.

If your sensory system is flagging, if you want to enjoy a close relationship with someone again, you'll need to revive and refresh your mind and body. Don't project your ex-partner's faults onto every new person you meet; some innocent comment may trigger memories that make us too self-protective. And drop your medicators. Each one of us has a medicator that "helps" us forget our emotional hot spots. If you hunger for a healthy relationship with someone, make that someone yourself first. Then you will have maximized your chances for success in the next partnership.

I have many concerns and much sadness for the people who look for intimacy while they are still smoking, drinking, overworking or exercising to excess. It is impossible to reach intimacy while we are medicated. So, first, all medicators have to go! This is a reality test. Are you truly interested in intimacy? Or do you want a new kind of person in your life while holding onto the same mentality that attracted and maintained the old relationship? The choice may be easy but doing it may take real desire.

Second, we have to find ways to express our feelings more deeply and more often. Newness can encourage us in this activity. Try new things, see new or old things in a new light; go new places.

Analyze a painful feeling and see where it leads. Both painful and joyful feelings open us up to new awareness and understanding. That's what forms us into the kind of people who have something to contribute to intimacy.

Feelings are frightening for a person who hasn't had them for a while or who has tried not to have them. Giving up our medicators lets our feelings surface. Try enjoying them in the emotional intimacy of physical closeness without intercourse. It is not necessary to have sex every single time we become physically affectionate, close or emotional with each other. An understanding partner will let us become comfortable with this physical/emotional closeness without sex.

After we have achieved progress in our own personal recovery, then we can begin to look at what it means to achieve recovery in a relationship. That takes some renegotiation. "How much of my time am I going to spend on me, personally, and how much time am I going to spend getting used to closeness?"

Relationships are a choice. Intimacy is a choice. Both are choices we can make, but then we need to commit time, energy, willingness and integrity to that process.

How Much Time Does Intimacy Take?

Finding the right kind of sexual experience isn't like finding a pretty stone on the beach. People actually have to carve out time to create it. Those who do are the people who rate their relationships very high on their list of important things in life. Many of the people who have achieved a highly satisfying sex life, report that they spend at least 75 percent of their nonworking hours with their mates.

Many of us have been conditioned to feel that the more we *do*, the more we *are*. This philosophy won't help our relationships at all. We have only one taskmaster. That is us. We're the ones who make commitments that reduce our personal time to a half-hour at night. Some people need to fit their commitment to their partner in with their exercise, housework, classes or hobbies. After a divorce takes place, people want to make sure that they have quality time with their children. Add all of that up and pretty soon there is no time for partnering. That brings us to the issue, "Do I want a close relationship or don't I?"

If it's "I do," then it will take some time to devote to a second marriage or serious long-term relationship. When you do that, you may have to let some other activities go. Maybe the house will be a mess once in a while. Maybe the class won't be attended with as great a commitment. Maybe the fitness club will be visited twice a week, instead of five times a week.

Many people are coming to realize that we can't have it all, and in the 1990s, relationships need extra-sensitive treatment. If the relationship is going to work, and if it's going to be good, it will have to be a priority, which takes commitment and energy.

For a long time in marriage and intimacy counseling, there was the saying, "Before you can love anyone else, you have to be able to love yourself." That statement is still true, but now we hear another saying, "You will only be complete as you learn to love another." You cannot be completed *by* another, but when you acquire the capacity to be close, you will feel more fulfilled. Fear of intimacy and commitment is being recognized as a real impediment to personal growth.

We're not saying everybody has to go out and have a second relationship. Not everybody is going to want to do that. But there are many people for whom having a clear, close, satisfying relationship is a very important ingredient in their emotional and physical health. Does this mean that if you decide to stay single you are destined to stay or become psychologically troubled? Of course not!

HAPPY SINGLEHOOD

Enjoying living alone is also an important trend in the '90s, and there are many, many ways besides marriage to learn to love someone or learn to connect meaningfully with others. We can learn to be very discriminating in our closest relationships and make sure that the intimate friendships we choose, regardless of the sex involved, are between strong, mutually respecting equals.

There are many people who, once they have been single, begin to grow in their own right. They thrive on the enjoyment of good friends, a rich life and being in charge of themselves and their own time. One disadvantage is that other people often can't leave them alone and ask, "How come you're not married?" Listed below are several reasons you can give to vary: "I don't want to be!"

1. I haven't been asked.
2. Arnold Schwarzenegger is very happy with Maria Shriver, and I won't settle for less.
3. I don't have the right dress.
4. Just lucky, I guess.
5. I still haven't given up a shot at the "Miss America" title.
6. I only earn enough frequent flyer tickets for one.
7. I'd have to forfeit my trust fund.
8. I'm married to my career.
9. I haven't your nerve.

Whether we want to stay single or not, singlehood is far superior to staying in a painful marriage. Singlehood gives us the room to grow unfettered in peace with no limits to our potential for self-created happiness. Divorce in this country is a stigma in very few places. Americans are famous for their practicality. If something doesn't work, fix it. If it can't be fixed, find something that does work. No intelligent person imagines divorce is the easy way out of a painful relationship, but it is often the only way to give our personhood and our sexuality the chance for healthy expression.

CHOOSING REMARRIAGE

Aside from any children you might have, the greatest gift your ex-spouse might have given you (unintentionally!) is a firm sense of what you *don't* want in your next marriage. We all pretty much know the qualities we'd like to find, but there's nothing like a divorce to make it crystal clear what changes we want in our relationships.

So perhaps you would like to remarry. Undoubtedly, you're especially interested in not making a mistake. The presence of certain qualities in a person can reassure you that, this time, you are on the right track. The candidate who seems to be the most respectful of your differences — not just your similarities — in one another, is most likely not to disappoint. This would also be someone who:

- Would say "I love you" spontaneously.
- Would be patient with you as you try to make it in a new marriage.
- Knows what he/she wants out of life and is willing to work for it, and who is also willing to let you do the same, in your own way.
- Is affectionate.
- Doesn't want to change you and accepts you the way you are.

Figure 10.5. Loving Relationships

Loving Relationships

*L**ove is a friendship that has caught fire. It is quiet understanding, mutual confidence, sharing and forgiving. It is loyalty
through the good times and bad. It settles for less than perfection
and makes allowances for weaknesses.*

*Love is content with the present, it hopes for the future, and
doesn't brood over the past. It's the day in, day out chronicles of
irritations, problems, compromises, small disappointments, big
victories and common goals.*

*If you have love in your life, it can make up for a great many
things you lack. If you don't have it, no matter what else there is,
it is not enough.*

Author Unknown

- Will work with you in resolving issues around *his* children, *her* children, *our* children or *no* children.

HAPPY REMARRIAGE "SECRETS"

Frequently, couples who have been married a zillion years are asked "What is your secret?" The happy pair may have narrowed their response down to something like "We never go to bed angry!" but it really takes a lot of "secrets" to make a marriage a success.

Someone has said, "Happiness is spending more time building relationships than worrying about losing them." With that in mind, here are ten "secrets" for a happy re-marriage:

1. You know you are probably on your way to a healthy relationship if you immediately feel some sense of "being at home" with each other. Elementary to a lasting relationship is some sense of rapport, comfortableness and ease.

2. A couple must share honor and respect for one another. Even when you think your mate is wrong or completely offbase, you don't lose faith that at their core is honesty, fairness and commitment. Long-lasting lovers always give each other the benefit of the doubt. If both of you feel that way, you probably have a solid foundation for your life together.

3. If the other's happiness is high priority, if you desire with all your might that your partner succeed, do well at work, live and play in health — that's a good sign. There is something about your partner that has touched you profoundly. Wanting happiness and health for your mate, from the bottom of your heart, is a sign that you already love your partner.

4. Couples that are going to make it probably have lots of similarities and lots of differences. Their similarities provides a sense of comfort and ease, a tranquil ability to live with each other, day in and day out, through the ups and downs, and joys and traumas of life. Their differences

provide excitement and challenge. Their different hobbies, different friends and different outlooks on life enrich the relationship.

5. Couples really wanting to make marriage work, face their problems and don't carry resentments. Each day is too short to stay angry, to indulge in the "silent treatment" or to nurse resentments. Breakfast is a great togetherness time of sharing coffee, maybe reading some meditation books and then separating for the day. But, oh, what an exciting day when you know that in the evening, you each have a haven to return to — a little time together, a little candlelight, and being able to share the day's adventures with someone who cares. There is a sense of comfort that neither partner wants to muddy with grudges. When you know that what you have together is more than what you have with anyone else, you are well on your way to a long and happy relationship.

6. You aren't afraid of having routines. Some people think routines are boring and others think they are a part of inner peace. If you enjoying sharing routines or find more inner peace with your partner, you've probably found the right mate. Routines, in many ways, suggest trust and confidence. Although routines are shortcuts to happiness, they don't produce it, but they do enhance the ability to trust your partner. They also become a very necessary part of a healthy relationship.

7. There is some kind of a life dream. Life dreams can be very short, like "Let's save everything we've got and take a trip to Europe next fall!" Or, "Let's save for three years and buy ourselves that house in the country that we always wanted to have." Or, "Maybe if we both work hard for a year or two we will have the kind of stability that we'd like to have. Maybe we wouldn't have to work so hard." Your dreams could be wanting to work in such a way that you could retire at an early age. Or maybe write a book or start a business together. It really doesn't

matter much what the dream is. What counts is a common underlying desire and excitement about life. Maybe there's even something the two of you could do together that one probably wouldn't attempt alone.

People who share dreams tend to enjoy remarkably happy marriages, much happier than most. Whatever the content of the dream, it's the sharing and joint effort towards it that make a couple feel a lot of fulfillment.

8. A major indicator of a happy couple is that they learn to roll with the punches. Nobody has an easy, well-laid-out life that just unfolds without any kind of trauma or stress. There are all kinds of things that come up. Many things can occur that work against the relationship, too, such as problems with a job, finances, adult children or in-laws. There are also many stresses on a marriage. Partners must decide very early, "Do we want a coupleship or don't we?" If they do, they must "roll with the punches" as they work out the coupleship.

It is very important for a couple to have certain principles they will both stand by. Basically, they must protect the marriage against all outside invasion. Many marriages have been torn apart by outside influences, such as painful relationships with children, "ex-anythings," job stress and financial difficulties. The couple needs to decide how important the relationship is, and if it is important, both partners' actions will support its survival.

9. The importance of sex and romance is not underestimated. Usually sex and romance have been what brought the couple together in the first place. It's the glue that keeps the partners focused on the coupleship. A good partnership rests upon the cherished qualities of daily intimacy: touching, hugs, comments like "I love you" and daily respect. Many couples will need to learn how vital it is to sneak away to movies, take long weekend vacations or possibly go on ones that are very far away, buy little gifts or cards for one another, light candles,

share in kitchen chores or plan surprises for each other.

There are so many things couples can do to enhance their relationship. You might take a look at my book *Coupleship* (Health Communications, 1988) for ideas on how to enhance romance within a marriage. If you scratch underneath the surface of a happy marriage, you will find a real chemistry and commitment to making it an exciting partnership.

The miracle of a coupleship full of meaning is that even though these people have an exclusive relationship, seeing each other day after day, boredom doesn't set in. Instead, the more that is added to romance and sex, the stronger the foundation of the partnership becomes. As life moves on and we move with it, our attraction to each other becomes greater, not lesser. There seems to be an interacting chemistry, a strong force that bonds people together throughout the years.

10. Couples who really make it in a relationship that fulfills both their needs, do believe in and practice monogamy. In all my work with families and couples, plus the surveys that I have done, monogamy is one of the most important factors in a coupleship. Being faithful is not just something one chooses to do. Being faithful, for happy couples, is the foundation upon which the marriage was built. It was a basic requirement.

When I began interviewing people on the subject of happy marriages, I had planned to accumulate quite a large variety of opinions on fidelity, its pros and cons, and where it fits into a good relationship. But as I interviewed people, they simply said, "Well, yes, of course, we always expected fidelity." Couples who are able to make marriage fulfilling and satisfying simply do not even entertain the idea of an "open marriage" or multiple partners. Couples who contemplate meaningful relationships and are capable of achieving them, seem to begin with this given: Monogamy is the only way to go.

Figure 10.6. Dance

Remember to let the winds of heaven
dance between you.

— *Ralph Blum*

11

Mapping Your Journey Of Change

Divorce often leaves us feeling powerless but, as we have shown here and in one of my previous books, *Choicemaking*, we don't have to be victims. Although our ability may become obsured by emotion at times of crisis, we never lose the power to change our lives for the better.

As we renew our efforts to make healthy moves in our own and in our loved ones' interests, we observe that we can make successful decisions again. Anyway, being 100 percent "right" in life is a capacity of perfection that no one enjoys. Not many of us can even predict how we'll change, much less how our spouses will change. So, full of forgiveness for our own shortcomings and others, we find our new way through a new life, brimming with exciting possibilities.

Following a divorce we are eager to start planning for the future. Then we realize that along the way, in a marriage with many demands (perhaps including those of our children), we've neglected to stock some of the tools we need for self-sufficiency. Maybe we were borrowing others'. Now, though, we recognize some of the capacities that we need to boost our lives forward. They may include the ability to listen, share thoughts and feelings, decide on some healthy new commitments that make us feel good, and learn when and how to ask questions.

Most importantly, our recovery months are the time to find out how to trust, rest, reflect and make changes. They are a period in which we have been challenged to simplify and reach some inner peace. After all this, do we get to lean back and cruise on our life's journey? No way! The biggest changes, possibly the hardest ones and those with the greatest rewards, are yet to come!

During this time of self-supportive care, you have been preparing for the most important phase of recovery: The commitment to keep it going, to make self-care, self-development and self-discovery a continuing effort in your life. Establishing a set of goals will focus you on that promise to yourself.

WHAT ARE YOUR PRO-SELF RIGHTS?

One of your prime goals should be to remember to assert your rights at every opportunity. This may take a great deal of practice, but practice will give you confidence in the necessity of living your own life. Many people think the choices they may make are their own until they review a basic list of human rights, such as:

1. You have a right to say no to anything that violates your values.
2. You have a right to say no to requests that conflict with your priorities.
3. You have a right to stand up for yourself.
4. You have a right and an obligation to honestly share your feelings.
5. You have a right to change your mind.

6. You have a right to seek healthy feelings and behaviors from others.
7. You have a right to make mistakes.
8. You have a right to your own program of recovery and healing.

Divorce recovery is possible for those who can make changes.

GROWING HEALTHY THROUGH CHANGE

For someone who has been watching and waiting for the approval of others, weighing alternatives without acting, stalling in fear or being paralyzed with concern over making mistakes, choicemaking is a difficult task. As we enter divorce recovery we often expect too much of ourselves too soon. Growing healthy means taking more and more responsibility for every area of life, but this good feeling won't come overnight. There are going to be some mistakes, some false starts, some hesitation and falling back to gain strength. Push yourself, but don't push yourself down. To learn to swim you have to learn to float first. But in order to learn to float, you have to let go of that familiar bottom of the pool and lean into the water. We have to give ourselves up to something that, at first, feels as if it won't support our weight. But life is supportive; that's its job!

SURRENDER

As we move forward on our path, we will find ourselves repeatedly in situations that will require learning and relearning the value of acceptance and surrender. The dictionary defines surrender as the "giving up of one's position." Here's my definition, a little bit more elaborate, of what I've found surrender to be:

1. *Surrender* means not being protective of other people, but to let those you love face their own reality.
2. *Surrender* means to stop controlling others, and to start using your energy to become what you dream yourself to be.
3. *Surrender* is to accept and not regret the past which is done and over with. It is to grow, plan and live.
4. *Surrender* is to stop playing games with oneself, to stop denying and to start seeing things as they are.
5. *Surrender* means to stop being in the middle of a raging and controlling event. It is to let go.
6. *Surrender* is to celebrate victory!

The victory of recovery does not come easily. It is preceded by many losses, goodbyes, times of loneliness and sometimes fear. There are many things to think about and, often, too little time. There are new thoughts and new questions. Yet you know you're on the right path because of the moments of inner peace and inner comfort that are beginning to occur more frequently.

Becoming a choicemaker and freeing yourself from emotional bondage allows you to start your passage away from anxiety. When we look back at our marriage from this vantage point, we may see that for some time it was a stagnant pond, familiar yet not too healthy. If you dam up a river, it will die. Life must move on. What is most natural for people, too, is to live and to grow, and not cling to the status quo.

RECOVERY PITFALLS

The good feelings and growth you will begin to experience in recovery will be necessary to sustain you as you re-enter and renegotiate new situations. In this process you will encounter some pitfalls that are important to skip across so your recovery doesn't stall. Here are the most important recovery pitfalls:

1. *Clinging to resentment.* Resentment will bring us back to negativity. Forgiveness and understanding is a part of healing.
2. *Secret recovery.* Downplaying the joy of recovery dilutes it. It's important to share your excitement with family and friends.
3. *Recovery guilt.* Not embracing the fullness of recovery because we feel sorry for those who are still hurting makes us vulnerable to relapse and retreat; this is self-sabotage.
4. *Fear and avoidance.* Knowledge that doesn't lead to action only brings about frustration. We don't need frustration in divorce recovery. To know we need to make a change and actually changing are two different things. We can't bridge the gap with fear and avoidance. Only action brings about newness in our lives.

RELAPSE SYMPTOMS

If we become mired in any of these pitfalls, we run the risk of prolonged relapse or stagnation in our growth. We need to pay special attention to the following symptoms of possible relapse. Enlist the help of those close to you as lookouts for any of these symptoms. It is much easier to prevent a relapse than to recover from it. Symptoms of possible relapse are:

1. *Fatigue.* This results from allowing yourself to become overly tired or careless about your health. Workaholics, especially, try to do too much too fast in recovery.
2. *Frustration.* Feeling thwarted is only a sign that we're not expressing appropriate anger.
3. *Impatience.* We find ourselves short-tempered when we try to take control again.

12 STEPS BACK TO RECOVERY

If you feel any of these symptoms occurring with regularity, there are some steps you can take to get back into recovery:

1. Make a commitment to seek outside help from a therapist.
2. Ask someone who cares about you for an opinion of how you're doing — and listen to it.
3. Stay with the truth. (No fibbing, understatements or white lies.)
4. Make obvious decisions.
5. Take responsibility for yourself.
6. Get some exercise and take care of your body.
7. Choose friends carefully. Misery loves company but it may not be the best company. Surround yourself with people who have positive attitudes.
8. Accept some down hours and days. Living in sunshine without rain stunts growth.
9. Learn something new. Knowledge is power.
10. Heal family rifts wherever possible. Good family friends are a wonderful support system.
11. Take plenty of time to be quiet and alone. As we continue to know ourselves and spend time with ourselves, we heal.
12. Expect and recognize wonderful surprises. Over time, they will become more frequent.

Risk and choicemaking may not be easy, but, if you risk nothing, nothing will be gained. The greatest block to recovery is to risk nothing. You may avoid short-term discomfort or suffering, but you will also block learning and feeling, changing and loving, and any kind of a full, exciting life. That is the forfeiture of human feeling.

Only the person who risks becomes free.

THE RAINBOW CHECK-UP

The rainbow has long been a good-luck sign in the life of humankind, representing balance, beauty and prosperity. Such is the mystical, luminous beauty that we have long speculated that rainbows begin and end in spots very fortunate, containing great wealth or the proverbial pot of gold.

For many years I was active in a spiritual community called "The Cursillo." One of our special symbols of joy and balance was another multi-colored entity, the rooster, again signifying the richness of a balanced life.

A way to keep track of how much color and brightness you are bringing to your own life is to chart your self-care monthly with "My Rainbow Color Wheel." Purchase a fresh new set of colored markers, and at the end of the month evaluate your wheel. You can make several copies of this page and fill in the different colored bands to represent responsibility you have taken for yourself. As you accumulate these records, you will gain confidence seeing your life become more colorful and rich.

FROM THE OLD, THE NEW

What may feel like an end may just be the "darkness before the dawn," and that dawn may be a new idea, a new possibility, a new challenge or a new person. You have within you the power to turn your terminations into transitions, and your transitions into new beginnings.

Sometimes when we think we have to start all over again, we moan, "Oh, my God, I've wasted all of my history, all of my past and all of my experience." That is a myth stemming from our insecurity. Rarely has any of our past been in vain or been wasted.

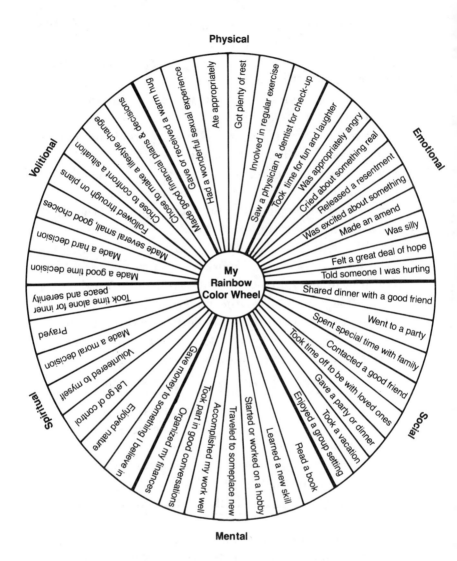

Figure 11.1. Rainbow Wheel Art

Our feelings are our sixth sense. It is this sense that interprets, arranges, and directs and summarizes the other five. Our feelings tell us whether we are experiencing threat, pain, regret, sorrow, joy or fear. Feelings make us human. Feelings make us all siblings. Because so much of what we know depends on our feelings, to not be able to feel them, identify or talk about them, or to be confused by them, is to be overwhelmed by the world. Understanding feelings is the key to mastering ourselves and finding much of our own personal power.

If you allow yourself to experience the natural stages of emotional hurt and do not try to avoid reality, you will be able to resolve your pain and you will heal. Your energy will return and so will your clarity. The practice of facing and solving emotional problems strengthens our ability to achieve real growth and development in life. Otherwise, the unresolved issues of our childhood and of our later crucial experiences will continue to reappear as conflicts in our lives and continue to shape us in ways we don't want. We can see the purposeful pattern of those who are serious about claiming their share of happiness in life through self-understanding. They move from dependency to independence to mastery to freedom.

If we are closed, we will waste our energy and never attain our potential.

If we remain open to new ways of thinking and being, we will grow.

If we can dream it, we can do it. Courage plus commitment plus action result in the confidence it takes to make dreams happen.

Every ending is a new beginning.